Living Alone

New Library of Pastoral Care
GENERAL EDITOR: DEREK BLOWS

LIVING ALONE

The Inward Journey to Fellowship

Martin Israel

First published 1982
SPCK
Holy Trinity Church
Marylebone Road
London NW1 4DU

Second Impression 1983

Acknowledgements
Unless otherwise stated, biblical quotations in this book are from the
New English Bible, second edition © 1970, and are used by
permission of Oxford and Cambridge University Presses.

British Library Cataloguing in Publication Data

Israel, Martin
    Living alone.—(New library of pastoral care)
    1. Single persons—Religious life
    I. Title   II. Series
    261.8′3588   BV4596.S5

    ISBN 0-281-03854-6

Filmset by Pioneer
Printed in Great Britain by
The Anchor Press, Tiptree.

Contents

Foreword

The *New Library of Pastoral Care* has been planned to meet the needs of those people concerned with pastoral care, whether clergy or lay, who seek to improve their knowledge and skills in this field. Equally, it is hoped that it may prove useful to those secular helpers who may wish to understand the role of the pastor.

Pastoral care in every age has drawn from contemporary secular knowledge to inform its understanding of man and his various needs and of the ways in which these needs might be met. Today it is perhaps the secular helping professions of social work, counselling and psychotherapy, and community development which have particular contributions to make to the pastor in his work. Such knowledge does not stand still, and pastors would have a struggle to keep up with the endless tide of new developments which pour out from these and other disciplines, and to sort out which ideas and practices might be relevant to his particular pastoral needs. Among present-day ideas, for instance, of particular value might be an understanding of the social context of the pastoral task, the dynamics of the helping relationship, the attitudes and skills as well as factual knowledge which might make for effective pastoral intervention, and perhaps most significant of all, the study of particular cases, whether through verbatim reports of interviews or general case presentation. The discovery of ways of learning from what one is doing is becoming increasingly important.

There is always a danger that a pastor who drinks deeply at the well of a secular discipline may lose his grasp of his own pastoral identity and become 'just another' social worker or counsellor. It in no way detracts from the value of these professions to assert that the role and task of the pastor are quite unique among the helping professions and deserve to be

vii

clarified and strengthened rather than weakened. The theological commitment of the pastor and the appropriate use of his role will be a recurrent theme of the series. At the same time the pastor cannot afford to work in a vacuum. He needs to be able to communicate and co-operate with those helpers in other disciplines whose work may overlap, without loss of his own unique role. This in turn will mean being able to communicate with them through some understanding of their concepts and language.

Finally, there is a rich variety of styles and approaches in pastoral work within the various religious traditions. No attempt will be made to secure a uniform approach. The Library will contain the variety, and even perhaps occasional eccentricity, which such a title suggests. Some books will be more specifically theological and others more concerned with particular areas of need or practice. It is hoped that all of them will have a usefulness that will reach right across the boundaries of religious denomination.

DEREK BLOWS
Series Editor

Preface

This book is dedicated to those many people who, perhaps because of some physical impediment or social misfortune, are obliged to live alone. The experience can be shattering if a deeper spring of personality is not unveiled within and a more profound meaning to life revealed. It is a fearful sensation to feel cut off from one's associates on a deeper social level, because one can hardly escape the suspicion that there must be something radically wrong with oneself that one has had to embark on a solitary mode of existence.

In fact, all experiences bring us closer to the core of reality within us if we have the courage to persist on the path. The celebrated Socratic injunction that we should know ourselves is the path of all wisdom. But it must be prefaced with the biblical dictum that the fear of God is the beginning of that path. A period of separation from the complacent reassurance of worldly society is a most potent way of arriving at that appreciation of God's providence and the deeper knowledge of the self. Indeed, it is open to doubt if there is any other way towards this understanding.

Living alone is a very individual experience. Each one treads it according to his own gifts, insights and temperament. But one fact stands out: until one has come to terms with one's own personality and has attained an inner rest in the silence of aloneness amid the outer turmoil of the world, all one's gifts are inadequate to assuage the loneliness, indeed the meaninglessness, of one's present existence. This book explores the inner life of a person with special reference to living on one's own. It outlines the path to awareness that finds its end in the direct encounter with God. It is to this end that man was fashioned. It is first glimpsed in the silence of aloneness, but it is finally consummated in a truly communal life that is the fruit of a period of living alone well spent and fully used.

Accustom thyself to the holy service of this inward temple. In the midst of it is the fountain of living water, of which thou mayest drink, and live for ever. There the mysteries of thy redemption are celebrated, or rather opened in life and power. There the supper of the Lamb is kept; the bread that cometh down from heaven, that giveth life to the world, is thy true nourishment: all is done, and known in real experience, in a living sensibility of the work of God on the soul. There the birth, the life, the sufferings, the death, the resurrection and ascension of Christ, are not merely remembered, but inwardly found, and enjoyed as the real states of thy soul, which has followed Christ in the regeneration. When once thou art well grounded in this inward worship, thou wilt have learnt to live unto God above time, and place. For every day will be a Sunday to thee, and wherever thou goest, thou wilt have a priest, a church and an altar along with thee.

from *The Spirit of Prayer* by William Law

ONE

The Life Apart

One basic experience that unites all people is an inner aloneness. Even when one has become immersed in the hectic thrust of conviviality, there remains an inner core of foreboding sensitivity that is shrouded by a cloud of diffidence. A dark threat of exposure hangs over our inner life, which is liable to be violated by the unfeeling, uncomprehending gaze of the hostile outer world. When the outer show of social life is disrupted by the inroads of distress and loss, the companions of one's pleasure depart and one is left painfully alone. This is the moment of truth, that one can ultimately rely on no other person, that the seed of one's salvation lies within oneself alone.

In the Genesis story, God, having created man and all the other creatures of the world, says of the man Adam: 'It is not good for the man to be alone, I will provide a partner for him.' Since no partner adequate for human company is found among any of the creatures, God creates the woman Eve from the man's substance. She is brought to the man who acclaims her as bone of his bone, flesh of his flesh. This is why a man leaves father and mother and is united to his wife, and the two become one flesh. In the beginning both were naked and felt no shame towards one another (Gen. 2.18−25). In the account of the Fall in Genesis 3, as soon as the human has elevated his own will and intelligence above that of God and has assumed independence of judgement so as to make moral decisions for himself, he is separated from his wife and indeed from the whole of nature. The eyes of both of them were opened so that they discovered their nakedness. Being ashamed, they made loin-cloths for themselves by stitching fig-leaves together. Thus separation has cleaved the natural unity of life, and a predatory concern for personal well-being has replaced a childlike unconscious trust in the all-encompassing providence of God. From henceforth man

1

proceeds on his journey alone even when surrounded by his peers. He finds himself banished from the primeval heaven where he had lived in heedless bliss, and he has now to tread a hard, solitary path towards the realization of his true nature and destiny. Where once there was peace and full communion with life, there is now rivalry for the earth's resources, hatred and death. The essentially solitary nature of unredeemed humanity has been proclaimed. This is the human condition; it is the life apart from fellowship in God, and it cannot be transcended, let alone abolished, by any scheme of human endeavour or co-operation that does not take into account the divine aspect of human nature. To quote St Augustine's famous words that introduce his *Confessions:* 'You have made us for yourself, O God, and our souls are restless till they rest in you.' When the full significance of this profound analysis of the human condition is finally grasped, a completely new dimension to the situation of living alone in the world is shown to us. Instead of being simply a morbid condition to be cured by specious social manipulation—or what is often called 'do-gooding'—it becomes an authentic way of life, fraught with difficulties and dangers that have to be faced with courage and resourcefulness, which promises the birth of a new person as its end.

The life apart for any person starts at the day of separation from the mother's womb, when the intimate contact of the enclosing organism is finally disrupted. When the child leaves its home to enter school the separation widens—not only for the child but also for its parents. The close, intimate contact of a caring group—assuming the home situation has been good—is replaced by the fragmentary confrontation of a selection of peers and teachers, who, even if kind and solicitous about the individual's welfare, have their own lives to lead and their own problems to untangle. At the end of the period of schooling the young adult is thrust out into the wider world, leaving childhood impressions rapidly behind him, as he battles his way through the open competition of the society into which he is thrust. To be sure, he may be one of those privileged to share the environment of learning and mutual support and aspiration of a university, but he is as likely to enter the life of a large city confined to a bed-sitter, finally alone and confronting his own identity fully for the

first time in his life. This experience of aloneness is one that
few adults can escape as they enter their chosen sphere of
study and employment. Even those who are accommodated
in an institution have eventually to fare for themselves in an
essentially impersonal situation of work, living on their own.

But man was not meant to be alone too much, hence the
biological urge towards friendship, marriage and the making
of a new home. In this way, the dull, insistent, but barely
acknowledged thud of inner discontent and foreboding is
effectively dulled by the surface diversion of material striving,
professional mastery, worldly success and affluence, and the
accumulation of possessions, be they people or things, which
occupy the attention to the exclusion of all else. The spiritual
paradox of this account of what the world would consider a
successful life is that it hardly uncovers the heroic depths
that lie concealed in even the most unpromising person. It is
in fact more an escape from a real encounter with life than
the pattern of desirable living. Fortunately for the progress of
the soul in each of us—that focus of inner authenticity that
makes itself felt in times of dilemma and moral choice—the
power above, whom we may call God or the workings of fate,
according to our own metaphysical view of reality, does not
leave us alone. The smooth course of even the best-ordered
life is in time disrupted by unexpected outer events that show
how superficial are the assumptions of worldly man, how
irrelevant are the plans of the socially well-ordered society in
the face of the vicissitudes of real existence. These vicissitudes
take the person away from the comfort of group living, single
him out and place him in a dry place of his own where, like
Job sitting on the ash heap, he can begin, perhaps for the first
time in his life, to recollect his past life and contemplate the
future alone. The type of event that leads to this enforced life
alone depends usually on the departure of someone on whom
the person had previously depended. The inescapable tragedy
of bereavement is the usual precursor of living alone in later
life, but nowadays the increasingly frequent breakdown of
the marriage relationship has added its complement to the
number of socially isolated people. In these instances women
are more often the victims than men inasmuch as it is easier
for a man than a woman to establish a new marriage
relationship. But this does not imply that men are more

fortunate than women in the ultimate experience of life, which means growing into spiritual maturity. As we shall see, it is only in the depths that truth is finally confronted and assimilated; the escape from darkness all too often also betokens an escape from a true encounter with the self, from which all truth is known.

Another circumstance that forces a person to lead an increasingly separate existence is chronic illness. This may be of a physical type, such as progressive arthritis or a neurological disease like multiple sclerosis. The chronically ill become an intolerable burden to their healthy relatives, and when these leave home, the indisposed have to care for themselves for long periods each day. There is also the dark experience of mental illness which all too effectively isolates the sufferer from the warmth of human affection. Many victims of mental illness are forced to live alone; even during a period of remission they may have little to do, and their life becomes increasingly burdensome and meaningless. Among any population of people destined to live alone for an indefinitely long period, a considerable number will be found to be mentally ill or have severe emotional problems. Some will be educationally retarded, so that the normal use of the mind which most of us take for granted will be denied them. It is evident from this very brief analysis of the extent of the situation that the range of people living alone is indeed vast. It extends from the contemplative saint whose life is devoted entirely to the benefit of his fellow men through prayer and service to the mentally and emotionally deprived person whose life balances precariously on the edge of moral collapse, crime and suicide. But even among this latter group of unfortunate people may be formed the nucleus of future sanctification of the human race.

And yet it must be emphasized that, although the experience of living alone is crucial for the development of an authentic personality, by which I mean a personality that can communicate in depth with the world and all its creatures, it is nevertheless equally true that man was not meant to be alone, as we have already seen in the Genesis myth. There is a great difference between *living* alone and *being* alone. The first is, as I have already stated, a necessary experience for coming to true maturity. The second is a tragedy which, if unrelieved, will end in death. Indeed it would not be inappropriate to define hell as an atmosphere of complete aloneness where there is an absence of communication with any other being. In such a state the comfort of God is not available; although he is most certainly present everywhere, his presence cannot be appreciated by those unfortunate persons immersed in the negative field of hell. But perhaps even the experience of hell on earth is a necessary precursor for the ultimate knowledge of God.

The privilege of being human is that one can think, reflect, contemplate, and grow in knowledge and attainment, even as Jesus did during the period that preceded his ministry. This growth in stature that is the very basis of human life takes place far more radically in times of adversity than during phases of success. Happiness may be the ideal for the worldly man; for the spiritually accomplished joy alone suffices, for it prevails even in the depths of gloom when all rational solutions are found to be futile. Living alone brings the person rapidly to the heart of the human condition, and from his strivings in the darkness, a new light is encountered. Its nature is meaning in obscurity.

TWO

The Experience of Aloneness

When one has, through the force of circumstances, to spend a period of time alone and separated from one's usual friends and associates, a vacuum suddenly appears in one's life. The immediate response is to fill it at all costs. There seems to be something wrong in being on one's own. Inasmuch as the image of a successful person presents itself as someone surrounded by friends, the centre of attraction and a figure of influence in the local situation, so the person outside life's immediate hustle and social activity is made to feel inferior if not psychologically disturbed. To admit that one is alone is the beginning of a great personal healing, to persist accepting that state of aloneness is the opening phase of a new dimension of living. To enjoy the silence of aloneness is the way to a deeper knowledge of God.

In this respect there is an important difference between aloneness and solitude. Solitude is a state that anyone can attain by an act of free choice. I, as the most sought-after person in the world, can escape from the crowds, as Jesus did in order to pray silently to his Father, and enjoy peace and quietness on my own. This is solitude, and is a prerequisite for an effective prayer life. When I have had my fill of tranquillity, I can resume the active social round once more, refreshed and renewed. The retreat movement, now a well-established part of spiritual development for the laity, is an obvious application of the principle of solitude. In this instance it is usually necessary for the retreatant's attention to be focused on the things of eternal truth by the Holy Spirit whose mouthpiece is the retreat conductor. Only those experienced in the spiritual life can find the Spirit of God within themselves sufficiently arresting to guide them in the adventure of inner silence. Otherwise the attention will wander ludicrously, and the person might as profitably be engaged in the commerce of everyday life as in wasting his time in wordless tumult.

By contrast, aloneness is thrust on the person by the circumstances of his life. The bastions of social support have been removed and he enters the nakedness of personal confrontation unshielded by all outer companionship. The result can be terrifying almost to the point of suicide if it is not rapidly relieved. In order to escape the terrible impact of truth that impinges on the naked soul, the person flees from one source of social activity to another, if he is what is generally called a 'normal' individual. He strives desperately to sustain the status quo by shallow conviviality or by interesting himself in some group activity, which may be educational, artistic or political. The end of this is not so much the education of the mind as the establishment of new associations that will be able to fill the threatening vacuum and allow the even flow of life to proceed. It is a fearful thing to fall into the void that is one's unfulfilled inner life, almost as terrible as falling into the hands of the living God that the writer of the Letter to the Hebrews describes. Indeed the two experiences touch each other; I will never know God until I know the inner hell of my unredeemed nature and the darkness that lies outside the cosy calm of intellectual assurance which I have until now identified with the whole of my life.

There is also a significant difference between aloneness and loneliness. The lonely person is depressed, unhappy and yearning for company. Yet there is something inside himself that seems to separate him from other people. It is, if it could be properly analysed, an inner feeling of inferiority, of unworthiness that robs him of composure and fellowship. One can be lonely even in the centre of a crowd of revellers or in a club of people sharing a common interest. This indicates that the root of loneliness lies far deeper than intellectual incompatibility. In the end we begin to realize that there is One who alone can satisfy the soul—God. Our hearts, as St Augustine reminds us, are restless until they are filled with his rest. Until we know the living God we will know neither ourselves nor our fellows. Shallow conviviality is the great deceiver. It directs our gaze away from the inner reality of dereliction by conjuring up a fantasy of fellowship based on a common interest. Loneliness indicates that the state of living alone has not been properly confronted and assimilated. It also tells us that there are ranges of our inner life that lie unexplored, being as yet shrouded in a dark pall of fear and meaninglessness. The writer of Psalms 42 and 43, a Levite exiled from the Temple in Jerusalem, complains of his depth of misery and groans in his distress, yet he will wait for God, praising him continually:

> Why so downcast, my soul
>   Why do you sigh within me?
> Put your hope in God: I shall praise him yet,
>   My saviour, my God.
>   (JB)

This verse, repeated on several occasions in the two psalms, voices the inner longing and unalleviated distress of the lonely soul. But whereas the Psalmist knows from whom healing alone can come, the lonely person is much more likely to search for relief by outer activities than by a courageous inner exploration of his true being in the state of aloneness.

Aloneness, unlike loneliness, accepts its situation and looks courageously into the future of a life apart from the immediate proximity of another person. It has its forbidding moments, but is also illumined with hope, the hope of a solid identity established and set firm in a raging sea of outer turmoil and destruction. When one can say through the bitter blows of impersonal outer events, 'Here I stand, and no mortal thing will move me from the centre of my being', one has indeed attained the stature of an adult. By comparison, many outwardly successful people who seem to be masters of their professions and emanate great charm, may contain within them a little child who has never grown up and has the childish qualities of exhibitionism, self-centredness and a complete unawareness of the needs of other people. How often do we meet apparently successful people who behave as spoilt children when they are in any way thwarted! By contrast, those who have explored their own depths can accept the vicissitudes of fate with equanimity and remain composed and even-tempered in the face of outer disaster or insult. The constructive use of silence is the key to a transformed character which no longer places itself at the centre of the world but rather sees itself as an expendable commodity for the use of all life.

What does it feel like to be left suddenly alone? If aloneness is thrust on one, the first reaction is to escape from it by seeking the company of other people. There is a round of telephone conversations followed by visits and shared entertainments, but soon this source of escape dries up. Other people have their own destiny to fulfil and their private interests take up their attention. One also learns how little in common one has, at least in the depth of one's personality, with one's so-called friends, who in fact are mostly superficial acquaintances. One also realizes how superficial one's own life has been, how it has depended for its sustenance on the support of other people whom one has seldom accepted in their own right apart from the use one can make of them. Whenever we are startled by the superficiality of those whom we once regarded as our friends, the finger of judgement is pointing as much at us as at them. It is our own previous lack of depth that is being starkly revealed.

And so the obsessive social round drives gradually to a halt when we have nothing further to offer those around us. The failing company of other people may to some extent be replaced by self-education in the form of reading many books, becoming interested in local political issues or joining societies devoted to learning, art or philanthropic endeavour. By this not only is the attention diverted from the immediate situation of aloneness, but even more important, there is the possibility and hope that new associations will take the place of the relationships of the past that proved so insubstantial when they were put to the test. It is indeed possible for the person who has to live alone to survive socially on this surface froth of encounters with people who share a common interest. But there is no depth, no true fellowship, by which I mean a sharing of the whole person, a mutual giving of selves to the edification of all.

Eventually one has to make the journey inwards. To be sure, this is not made voluntarily but is rather thrust on one. It is so forbidding that the dim intimations we have about it in normal consciousness when we are fully engaged in profitable work are speedily set aside by vain thoughts and fantasies about the future. One is reminded of the great rhapsody to wisdom in Job 28:

> 'Where then does wisdom come from,
> and where is the source of understanding?
> No creature on earth can see it,
> and it is hidden from the birds of the air.
> Destruction and death say
> "We know of it only by report."
> But God understands the way to it,
> he alone knows its source;
> for he can see to the ends of the earth
> and he surveys everything under heaven.'
>
> (verses 20—24)

We know of this inner realm of the self also by report alone; it is close to death and near to God, who is both our friend and lover and also a devouring fire. When we have to bear our own company for a considerable length of time, the darkness within becomes light visible as we explore the depths of our being.

This experience of aloneness with God—although few who are in the depths of life alone know that it is God who is with them—is the heart of a real retreat. But whereas the retreat has a finite duration and is usually made in the company of other people and in agreeable surroundings, the aloneness of common life has no set boundaries of time, but rather extends terrifyingly into the future, without limits and without end. It seems to point to a life of perpetual loneliness, exclusion from the company of one's fellows and stark purposelessness. In the depths of aloneness all one's fears are unleashed from their abode in the darkness of the unconscious mind and they enter into consciousness, empowered and magnified by the natural egoism of the unredeemed personality—by unredeemed I mean that the person is still a slave to the demands of his ego, which is the dictator within. To be redeemed from the slavery of sin, which is a vital concept of the spiritual life, means to be freed from the domination of the ego and enter into the service of all life under the protective love of God. It is in fact the journey, meaning and end of life.

The emergent fears that crowd into and dominate the awareness of the man who is left alone are all, in one way or another, related to his survival, or to be more precise, what he believes is necessary for his survival. Not too far from the surface of consciousness lie our true attitudes to our fellows. While there may be an outer affability, inwardly there is often a raging vortex of distrust, resentment and hatred against those whom we believe are scheming against us and seeking to destroy our livelihood, if not our life itself. This state of affairs, when consciously expressed, and provided, of course, it has no substance in fact, is called paranoia and is the preserve of the psychiatrist. But all of us have a submerged paranoid focus that is kept well under control, or repressed, while our outer circumstances are favourable. Once the situation changes and we are bereft of the usual human support, our repressed hatreds flare up and dominate us. All those who are apparently happy and well placed in their work are the source of our anguished envy. Soon we see how we have been used by others, taken advantage of and subtly diminished, while they have flourished at our expense. This, it need hardly be said, is a very dangerous psychological state, for it can alienate one increasingly from the small group of people around one who really do care. The sinister cults that batten on lonely, inadequate young people first succeed in separating them from their parents and close friends whom they portray as villains, set on thwarting their full develop-ment as independent people. When one is alone and not in contact with one's own inner centre, the most improbable suspicions concerning other people's malign influence on one's well-being start to ring true. Soon one is the victim of gigantic delusions of persecution and abuse so that the most harmless jest assumes the burden of a deadly insult. And so the mind paces around in circles of sterile thought about alleged past insults and the imaginary response one will deliver to the offenders when once one meets them again. Needless to say, if one does meet these associates in the flesh, all is calm and peaceful between oneself and them. The mind creates immense edifices of imaginary encounters and showdowns, but in the life of reality the structure collapses into a void. It is fortunate that this is the rule, otherwise serious damage might be done to those whom one mistakenly suspects of ill will and treachery.

It is easy to see how superficial is the good will we so often profess to those of a colour, race or religion different from our own. When all is going well we can afford to display *bonhomie* and 'tolerance' to those of different backgrounds. But when there is present trouble, the blame is soon projected from ourselves on to the stranger who cannot defend himself in an alien society. It is very important to recognize and understand this experience of latent xenophobia made manifest as the result of being alone. Many people who, quite rightly, speak against intolerance of this type are very unimaginative in their approach. They cannot enter into the depths of deprivation and fear of those who harbour destructive thoughts. Merely denouncing these antisocial attitudes does little good — it merely inflates the high opinion of the one who believes he is free of social prejudices, but who is probably as tainted as the one who gives vent to his distaste. Once one has been through this alarming disclosure of hatred, brought to light in the bleak climate of living alone, one can begin to act much more positively in countering such social evils as racial discrimination and religious intolerance.

The repressed hatreds that float to the surface of the person who is living alone are by no means limited to foreigners and rivals. They are directed also against siblings and parents who are inwardly accused of various wrong attitudes in the past that are believed to be the real cause of the present loneliness. It is all too easy to blame others for one's present unhappiness, especially as there is inevitably some basis of truth in such accusations. None of us is perfect, indeed the harder a parent tries to shield his children from difficulties, the more likely is he to interfere with the process of their growing up into full adulthood.

Unpleasant as all this is, it is far better that it should be exposed in full consciousness than remain partially hidden in the depths of the psyche only to emerge as episodes of hatred and malice when one is hurt or deprived later on. The things of darkness in ourselves have to be acknowledged clearly as our own particular cross to bear. Only then can they be inspected closely and dispassionately and put in their proper place. They are in fact a juvenile excrescence that has not been allowed to grow up into adult stature, so that it remains a split-off sub-personality. All of us contain within our depths tracts of past experience that remain poorly integrated into the full personality and persist instead as split-off portions of the psyche. These tend to invade the conscious realms of the psyche during dark periods of distress, and their influence can be truly demonic. It is often the successful, outgoing person who is especially liable to harbour these infantile residues in his unconscious, and he may have to undergo a radical inner reappraisal before there is real integration of the personality. The reason why this type of person is more liable to be immature in his depths than his more contemplative brother is because, in his striving for physical and intellectual proficiency (that typifies the man more often than the woman) he leaves a part of his psyche behind. He becomes a fully developed adult while remaining still essentially a youth; the outer hard face of the sophisticated grown man hides an emotionally and spiritually immature core that is subtly denied and ignored. In due course this unformed inner core makes its presence felt and then the outer edifice, so grand in appearance and distinguished to behold, collapses to reveal the child who has never grown up that lies concealed within. This inner child comes to consciousness when the outer façade of assurance and prosperity has been demolished by the inroads of disease, bereavement and loss of outer resources. At this juncture one is forced on one's inner resources, all outer support having been dramatically removed, and the dereliction that lies within is almost too terrible to bear. The sooner one does come to terms with it, however, the better is one's chance of starting afresh with a well-established inner centre and a newly fashioned personality.

Living alone exposes not only the depths of anguish and fear within one, but also the fantasy world in which one expends so much time in vain imaginings. These embrace all the qualities and attributes that one secretly covets but which are far from one's actual powers. In the sanctuary of one's own mind one can enjoy the acclaim that one longs for from one's contemporaries and bask in the acceptance that one has not fully known in one's life. And so the painful void of personal darkness is filled with illusory images of success and acknowledgement. This mechanism is one of escape from the threats of the dark, meaningless future, but it soon dissipates like an early morning mist, and leaves a stark landscape of dread to be faced in direct consciousness. Living alone, if it has no other advantage, does at least lead one into a direct exploration of one's mind and all the subterfuges it creates in order to deflect one from a proper confrontation of the reality of life. As the Hindu tradition reminds us, 'The mind is the slayer of the real'. It rationalizes and destroys spiritual experience if its destructive criticism is heeded too subserviently, and it also clothes the naked reality of the present with childish fears and imaginings. But the mind that acts in this subversive fashion is the reasoning, emotional power of the superficial ego. It is not the deeper understanding of the true self which is in contact with ultimate reality, since it is a part of that reality. Only when the true self is explored and its hidden wisdom tapped can we glimpse our future as people, and indeed envisage the destiny of mankind. In the experience of aloneness we are taken, provided we have the courage and determination to proceed, beyond the childish demands for instant satisfaction that characterize the ego, to the boundless realms of the true, or spiritual, self whose source and end is God. In this respect the ego can be defined as the immediate focus of self-awareness that claims for itself the full identity of the person. By contrast, the spiritual self is the whole range of the personality focused in a point of awareness that transcends the demands of the present. It effects a knowledge of eternal things, seeing the eternal reality in the present moment. The ego, on the other hand, tends to appropriate the present moment for itself, seeking self-satisfaction rather than self-identification with all life. The spiritual self is the centre or core of the person that is in communion with the Spirit of God. When it is articulated as a living reality, it transforms the ego so that this ceases to demand and starts to serve the person and the world. It becomes the instrument of the spiritual self.

In the intercourse of everyday life, we tend to communicate with the ego-filled mind, speaking *at* people rather than *to* them. This is because our attention is centred on ourselves, and what we really want of other people is that they should respond to us and share our own interests in life. We are all too seldom aware of others as independent individuals in their own right apart from ourselves and what we can get from them. What is rather speciously called fellowship often has the end result of separating us from our fellow men rather than bringing us closer together. We may find, to be sure, certain intellectual affinities with other people by virtue of a shared interest in, say, politics, art or a profession. But the true communication in depth that comes from the spiritual self—or the soul, as this self shows itself outwardly to us and to others—is actually occluded by the fictions of the mind. How easily I can separate myself from other people—and more disastrously still from my true self—by emitting a smokescreen of intellectual expertise or social polish! This façade passes quite plausibly for my true being to the uninformed. But underneath there lies the unfulfilled child longing for recognition and comfort. Until it is acknowledged there can never be an effective communication with myself; until I can communicate fully with my inner depths, I will not be able to relate properly to anyone else. These truths come closer to understanding through the experience of living alone. The fact is that until one is *at home in oneself,* one will never be *at home in the world.* And I can never be fully at home in myself until I am at home with God, who is nearer to me than my own sense of identity. God stands perpetually at the door of my soul and knocks so that he may enter. I am either not available to heed the knocking or else too much involved with the outer world to take notice. Until I am at home to receive the One who alone can fill me with the good things of eternal life, I remain empty even when crammed full of earthly dross, be it money, intellectual proficiency or the company of other people looking as obsessively as I for a way of escaping loneliness and despair.

The experience of living alone for any considerable period of time serves to show one how few inner resources one has on the surface level of existence. If I believe that now at last I will have time to do all the reading that I should like to do but for which I have never had the time or opportunity, I will soon become disillusioned. I will rapidly feel bored and dissatisfied. The accumulation of knowledge is of little value unless it can be put to use in the wider context of life. In other words knowledge, like money, has to circulate if it is to fulfil its purpose. If it is hoarded it turns stale and sours the personality. Likewise it will do me little good to spend my time listening to music or performing on an instrument if I am out of contact with the wider world. Art, even at its most noble and sublime, if it is used merely to keep my mind occupied, will soon lose its lustre and become increasingly dead to me. Literature, music and art find their place in directing me to the source of all wisdom, beauty and integrity, which is God. But that source cannot be found outside the community of living beings. Anyone who loves God as he ought, will discover quite spontaneously that he loves his fellow men also. No sphere of human endeavour that leads to the highest source can be secret or withheld from other people. Only in full participation with life do the benefits and joys of the arts shine out and lead one to a divine encounter. It follows therefore that the cultivation of some hobby or talent, though not without a certain basic value in lightening the dreariness of loneliness, will not succeed in overcoming it. It is therefore inadequate to advise a person suffering the isolation of a life alone to cultivate some diverting accomplishment. At most it takes his mind off the preoccupation with his present situation, but it leaves the fundamental problem unsolved. There has to be an inner change of life before the joys of creativity can be experienced and transmitted to others.

As one moves into the experience of living alone for an indefinite period, so one explores the various ways of escape into satisfaction of the self, only to find that each one is a cul-de-sac. People around one prove fickle and superficial in their affection, the practice of private skills leaves the inner void unfilled, and the workings of the mind lead one to a state that fluctuates between paranoia on the one hand and megalomania on the other, while in fact one moves deeper into a reactive depression as one sees an apparently unending road of loneliness lying ahead. This is the moment of truth: one can choose either life or death, transfiguration or suicide. At last one has come to the heart of the dilemma and also to the way of release from it.

THREE

The Secret Place

The title of this chapter is taken from the words Jesus used in teaching his disciples about prayer: 'When you pray, go into a room by yourself, shut the door, and pray to your Father who is there in the secret place; and your Father who sees what is secret will reward you' (Matt. 6.6). Like so much of Jesus' teaching, this has both a direct application, in which the words mean exactly what they say, and a deeper, more profound significance in which a more universal truth is enunciated. Both the direct and the deeper meanings are, of course, true in their own context and the one is not to be exalted above the other. Both have to be observed if prayer is to be valid. The room to which we have to retire before we can commune with God is, on the deeper level of under-standing, our true self or soul. Until we can claim entry into the depth of our being we will never be at home in ourselves. And until we are at home in ourselves, we will never be able to receive God, who knocks at the door and waits to be invited in (Rev. 3.20), and our fellow creatures. The end of the experience of aloneness is to gain a knowledge of the depth of our being, so that we can at last be at home in whatever situation we find ourselves. This is the recognition of the deep centre within where we can know peace in the face of the destructive fury of the outer world. It is only from the centre of being that we can rise above life's loneliness, which, as I have already pointed out, can be with us in the company of other people no less than when we are alone.

The discovery of the 'secret place of the Most High', which is primarily in the depths of one's own being, comes quite often during a moment of utmost dereliction. It can also come at the peak of an aesthetic experience when one is enraptured by great art or during the most intimate relationship with someone whom one loves very dearly. It is the Holy Spirit, the one who leads us into all truth, that shows us the way to the

spirit within us, and as Jesus taught Nicodemus, he blows
where he wills like the wind; one can hear its sound, but one
does not know where it comes from or where it is going
(John 3.8). But when the Spirit of God reveals the inner
centre at a moment of dereliction, the discovery is much more
likely to be long-lasting than when it comes with a peak
experience. The reason for this is that a peak experience, by
its very nature, can only be evanescent inasmuch as the
person soon comes down to earth after its glory. On the other
hand, when God reveals the inner centre during a period of
suffering, that experience will remain constantly in one's
memory as one returns once more to the vale of darkness.
One will remember that there is an inner sanctuary of peace
and radiance to which one can return, and eventually one will
take positive action to claim that sanctuary as one's own at
all times. This is where the disciplines of the inner life play
their part. When once the inadequacy of outer paths of
diversion has been finally grasped, the person on his own will
start to explore the inner way to self-sufficiency. The only
self-sufficiency that has a lasting reality is the communication
with that power of God within the person: 'Christ in you, the
hope of a glory to come' (Col. 1.27). Some translate this
sentence 'Christ among you' instead of 'Christ in you', and
this too is appropriate to our context, for when the inner
Christ is known, he is encountered also in the community
and in every face around us.

The initial encounter with the depth of one's being is, of
course, a gift of grace from God. It cannot be grasped
acquisitively from below. We are 'surprised by joy', as C. S.
Lewis points out, when we are least concerned with ourselves
and our ego-centred consciousness has been allowed to rest.
This is why peak experiences occur when one has been lifted
out of the narrow confines of personal striving by an encounter
of high aesthetic quality or an intense relationship with
someone deeply loved. The more one strives, the further the
ideal recedes, since the ego is seeking to possess that which
belongs to God alone. This was, in essence, the nature of the
primal sin of man, told mythologically in Genesis 3, and to
this day it is repeated by practitioners of the occult who strive
for paranormal powers while remaining ego-centred in their
attitude towards the creation and to God.

What steps then can we take to enter the inner sanctuary? We cannot force our way into it, for if we try to do so, the door is fastened and our entrance barred. We shall then either flounder about miserably in the depths or else be led sedulously into a false place whose edifice is composed of beguiling psychic images that may seduce the very elect into believing they have arrived at the centre where God is known. We move towards the centre of our being, paradoxically enough, by focusing our attention on the matters of immediate concern. We have to cultivate an awareness of the present place and time and be able to thank God (or providence, if we have no belief in the Deity) for the many blessings that are about us. De Caussade, in his spiritual classic *L'Abandon à la Providence Divine* ('Self Abandonment to the Divine Providence'), speaks of the sacrament of the present moment. If only we could give ourselves wholeheartedly to this very moment, we would see it, not in terms of a passing impulse of time, but as it really is, a mirror of eternity. Eternity, unlike perpetuity, is not an immeasurably long period of time, but rather the ultimate reality of God 'who was in the beginning, is now and ever shall be, world without end'. When we know eternity we know the real meaning and span of life, and we are made alive so that we can partake of the divine nature which is our birthright as well as our heritage. This knowledge comes to us as we give of ourselves freely to the present moment. It means that our mind must be focused on the eternal now, looking back neither to the past that cannot be altered, nor peering anxiously into the future whose vicissitudes can neither be predicted nor controlled. This does not imply an improvident way of life; it means living in the full intensity of the present, using all the gifts with which we have been endowed, and bestowing them without reserve on the world around us now. It means living so perfectly in the moment that we and the moment share a common identity, so that we and the world are one.

Jesus taught: 'You cannot serve God and Money. Therefore I bid you put away anxious thoughts about food and drink to keep you alive, and clothes to cover your body. Surely life is more than food, the body more than clothes.' He reminds us that the birds of the air do not accumulate food, and yet God feeds them. Anxiety cannot add a foot to the height of a human being. The flowers of the field are more beautifully arrayed in God's magnificence than human dignity at its most splendid. God knows our need for food and clothing, but the secret of abundant living is to set our mind on God's kingdom and his justice before everything else, and the rest will come to us as well. Do not be anxious about tomorrow, for it will look after itself. Each day has troubles enough of its own (Matt. 6.24—34). He reminds us also, in this context, that the body's lamp is the eye; if the eyes are sound, the whole body will be filled with light (verse 22).

To the crass and the worldly-wide these admonitions of Jesus seem impractical and remote. Much spiritual teaching has a similarly irritating effect on those who are weighed down with all the ills of this world—the crushing poverty of so many people and the terrible injustices that reduce whole populations to impotence. How can we reconcile this teaching about the sanctity of the present moment with the horror of the world and the need for material endeavour and planning? The answer lies in Jesus's own statement that the material blessings come to those who set their minds primarily on God. If one is fixed with one-pointed attention on the moment in hand, one's work will be so perfect that the requirements for life—food, clothing and much else besides—will be met. God works best through the alert, sensitive person at the height of his own powers. Thus it is that sound, singly focused eyes fill the body with light. By contrast, the wandering eye sees, in effect, nothing, since the person does not register the impressions that are conveyed to him by the restless, roving eye.

Jesus' teaching is neither visionary nor impractical. It is truly incarnational, revealing God's presence in the world. If only we ourselves could act as we were meant to, giving our whole attention to the work in hand, we would soon come to see how we were being sustained by a power far greater than that of the human mind. This is the power of the Holy Spirit, which perfects nature by grace, so that the image of God in which man was originally created is now restored undistorted and entire. At once the natural realm is raised to the dimension of the supernatural; alternatively nature at last attains its true stature. It mirrors the power and love of God in the created world.

All this is at the heart of the inner sanctuary of the soul, the secret place wherein we enjoy wordless communion with God. When we are fully engaged in the work of the present moment, the deeper consciousness enters unobtrusively into the secret place of the Most High, and at last peace has come to the whole personality. Stillness has come to us at the vortex of ceaseless activity, rest at the heart of agitation. This is, as I have already pointed out, a gift of God that cannot be appropriated by an act of will. But the will plays its part in the transaction by giving the whole person to God, 'as a living sacrifice', to do as he would have done. Thus we understand in a new light the famous words: 'Whoever cares for his own life is lost; but if a man will let himself be lost for my sake and for the Gospel, that man is safe' (Mark 8.35). The practice of the presence of God, to quote the title of Brother Lawrence's famous little book, is the heart of the spiritual life, and it is the only effective way by which a person who is obliged to live alone can emerge from the life-destroying images projected by the unquiet mind and enter a constructive calmness from which a new life can spring forth. This is the end of the experience of living alone: a new person has to emerge from the elements of the one whose old life was self-centred and vain. The old way spells doom; the new brings promise of a changed awareness of reality that is the harbinger of a completely alive person.

The place of psychotherapy can be seen in this context. While the mind is seriously unquiet because of the subterranean clamour of unresolved conflicts, the will cannot dedicate itself to the present moment. Its attention is at the mercy of every subversive complex in the unconscious, and as such it is rendered impotent. In this situation psychotherapeutic help may be necessary to unravel the emotional tangle that dominates the conscious life of the person. When this has, at least to some extent, been achieved, the Spirit of God can work unimpeded in that person, and at last the will is free to obey God, in whose service alone there is perfect freedom. But most people who are obliged to spend a length of time living alone do not need specialized psychotherapeutic help. The intelligence and courage can be harnessed to the Holy Spirit, who leads us all progressively into the full truth, sufficient at least for us to bear at the present moment. Life itself is the best analyst of the psyche, provided the person is psychologically strong enough to bear the revelations that the Spirit of God showers upon the conscious mind. Certainly there is no means more radical and complete of cleansing the person of all repressed illusions than a period of silence alone. A retreat performs this inner catharsis in pleasant surroundings and for a limited period of time; living alone has the same effect but much more starkly and radically. However, the end-result of living alone is not only self-sufficiency but also a growing ability to help other people in various kinds of difficulties. Once one has entered the secret place of one's own being, one soon learns that it is shared in common with all people. Inasmuch as God himself is known there, it is a 'place' of shared experience for all people. As St Paul reminds us, we are all members one of another. The experience of this common membership is in the secret place within. When I am at home here, I am always at home to all conditions of men, for I have penetrated beneath the selfishness of my ego to the depths of the soul. This is a gift beyond price of living alone and undergoing great inner privations. When I am nothing, I am in the company of the one who is always nothing for our sake, Jesus Christ crucified on the cross of human deceit and treachery. And then follows the resurrection of the full person into the light of God.

When all this theory is put into practice by the person who is obliged to live alone, it leads to a complete reappraisal of his attitude to his situation. Instead of trying desperately to escape into conviviality or outside activities, he learns to withdraw with determination and decisiveness ever more fully into himself and his limited environment. There should be no feeling of regret, let alone shame, in this attitude. One begins to see that one is fashioning a completely new type of existence for oneself in which one is master of the situation. It may be argued that this way of private life is easier for the person who is financially independent and whose surroundings are pleasant. But even if one is poor, one can still live decently in a small room if one loves that room. Some of the happiest people it has been my privilege to know have been elderly women who have been obliged to live alone in very confined quarters. Yet their home has been a place of delight to enter because it was always full of love and warmth. This love shows itself in the attention the person pays to the details of cleanliness and decoration and in the innocent beauty that emanates from the simplest arrangement of objects in the humble abode. It is worth remembering that even the richest person can sleep on only one bed at a time! Some of the most miserable, frustrated people I have known have lacked for nothing that money can buy, and yet they and their families have been continually at loggerheads, and their wealthy homes have been places of unhappiness and discord. It is a mistake to believe that living alone is necessarily less fulfilling than being at the centre of a large family, or that being confined to a single bed-sitter is inevitably soul-destroying. While it would be foolish to deny the benefit of space in allowing one to live more comfortably in a difficult situation, it is even more important to cultivate the inner space that leaves one free no matter where one finds oneself.

When one is young one may be fortunate enough to own a large house for oneself and one's family; when one is old even a small flat becomes something of a burden, and when one is preparing for the great adventure of dying, a single room with its bed seems a vast domain. And yet the dying person, if he has lived a constructive, self-giving life, knows a freedom that is hidden from his well-wishers and mourners. Freedom is a quality of mind that shows itself in one's attitude to life and possessions. It is reflected especially in one's home, even if this is a single room. Such a room becomes a sanctuary not only for the person who lives in it but also for the many people who visit it. And this is the end of living alone: to live in the deepest relationship with all kinds and classes of people drawn together by the bonds of love and mutual regard and not by superficial social usage. In one's depths one begins to see this gradual unfolding of the life ahead; it cannot be accelerated by an act of will, for it blossoms as slowly and beautifully as a bud, destined to open into a warm, glorious flower.

The way to the secret place which is our eternal home is by giving ourselves to the moment in hand and thanking God for that moment. It means an acknowledgement of all we have and are at that moment, which is the ever-present moment. This acknowledgement is not simply a mental registering of a fact, it is also a conscious sinking of oneself into the joy of the present experience. To be joyful that one is alive, that one has so many gifts of grace that are usually taken for granted — such as one's state of health, one's mental stability, one's inner integrity, that one has a means of support and that there are a few people who really do care about one — is the beginning of constructive living. Even if some of the causes for rejoicing that I have enumerated are lacking, there are surely others at least that are present. To be grateful for small mercies is the beginning of wisdom, for it reminds us of the providence of God.

As one relaxes in the gifts that surround one, so one's attention moves from fantasies and regrets to the ever-present moment. One starts to enjoy everything around one and then to enjoy one's own being. It is a sad reflection on the state of inner health of most of us that when we speak about enjoying ourselves, we automatically think of leaving our present situation and indulging in some form of diversion or entertainment. While there is nothing wrong in this — and indeed diversions and holidays are essential for the mental as well as the physical well-being of all of us — it is sad that we can so seldom find enjoyment in our own company. To have continually to seek enjoyment outside the periphery of our own being is a frank admission of our own inner bankruptcy. How much more satisfying it is to exult in one's body and soul, seeing in it something unique and unutterably wonderful, a cause for rejoicing to God the Creator! We remember the delighted cries of the Psalmist who writes: 'When I look up at thy heavens, the work of thy fingers, the moon and the stars set in their place by thee, what is man that thou shouldst remember him? Yet thou hast made him little less than a god, crowning him with honour and glory' (Ps. 8.3 — 5), and again; 'Thou it was who didst fashion my inward parts; thou didst knit me together in my mother's womb. I will praise thee, for thou dost fill me with awe; wonderful thou art, and wonderful thy works. Thou knowest me through and through: my body is no mystery to thee, how I was secretly kneaded into shape and patterned in the depths of the earth' (Ps. 139.13 — 15).

To enjoy oneself ought to mean enjoying being oneself, a unique creation of God unlike any other person, and yet finding one's true identity as part of the body of mankind.

But until one can articulate one's uniqueness alone and exult in it, one will never be able to contribute that unique spark to the world around one, and one will never be able to rejoice in the unique contribution that other people make to the whole. One can begin to appreciate and love other people — all people, not only those whom one believes are one's friends — only when one is so centred in oneself that one can flow out to them in joyful recognition as fellow seekers on the path of life. Then one ceases to judge them according to their age and sex, their cultural background and racial origin, their professional status and intellectual capacity, and instead accepts them joyfully for what they are in themselves. This, I am sure, is the way Jesus formed an instantaneous link with all those around him, though, of course, not everyone responded equally joyfully to his welcoming attitude. Those who were full of their own importance felt threatened by his open acceptance; those who were burdened with sin could, on the other hand, immediately feel lightened of that burden by contact with him. For he, though without sin, had such an intense sensitivity to all people, that he could identify himself with their sin and pain also.

As one gives of oneself to the present moment, so one suddenly becomes aware of a load being lifted from one. A lightness enters one so that the past fears, regrets and anxieties seem to fall away. 'Come to me, all whose work is hard, whose load is heavy; and I will give you relief' (Matt. 11.28), is the way this opening of the self to the Christ within reveals itself. When one knows this experience one has truly entered into the secret place of the Most High. At last one can rest fully in the eternal present and not need to look ahead for pleasure to come in order to assuage boredom and discontent. This state, let it be understood, is neither one of complacency nor of somnolence such as one might know after a heavy afternoon meal. One is fully awake, more emphatically oneself than ever before, and fully alert to the claims of the moment. But being centred in oneself, one can flow out from one's depths and be of assistance to anyone in trouble. One can respond as a fully live person to the calls of those in pain, being able first of all to listen, and then to take the appropriate action. One cannot listen until one is at home in the secret place, since it is only there that one is immutably fixed in will

and attention. When one is centred one can compose oneself
to listen to music and enjoy it, to read and gain the utmost
pleasure from what one imbibes. For now listening, reading
and performing are no longer actions undertaken to escape
from boredom and to evade loneliness. They are a direct
communion between oneself and the mind of the person who
created the music or wrote the book. This person is not only
the human mediator but also the Holy Spirit who is the
ultimate creative source of all that is good and noble.

It is important to distinguish between using literature and
art as a means of escaping from an encounter with the true
self, and of discovering from them the way to the creative
spark that comes from God. In the first usage one is separate
from what one reads or hears, and is in fact continually
aware of one's own isolation even when the word or form is at
its most beguiling. In the second encounter one is enabled to
transcend the awareness of one's own unhappiness and enter
a quite different realm of bliss, in the light of which one's
previous discontent pales into insignificance. As I have
stressed before, this bliss comes from God and cannot be
demanded or fabricated. But the one who gives of himself
wholeheartedly to the work will lose himself in it, only to find
his true being at the same time.

The end of living in the centre of one's being is that
everything around one is brought into that centre also. And
as it comes into the secret place within, so it is changed. It
ceases to be an object or a sensation apart from oneself, but
instead is transfigured into an aspect of divine reality deeply
set in the soul. One ceases simply to listen to music or to read
the written word. Instead the music and the word become a
part of one's life, indeed of one's very being. When this
experience is known and understood, the life alone ceases to
be depressing and meaningless; it takes on a joy and meaning
that transcend the limitations of time and space and bring
one in contact with all life.

FOUR

The Uses of Silence

Silence is spoken of proverbially as golden, yet only a few people would choose to possess it for more than a few moments. Silence is the way of communication of the soul with God; it is the wordless union that seals true fellowship. What is left unsaid in the heart is often much more authentic than what is communicated in words. Silence, however, is painful, even demonic, if it ceases to be a mode of communication. It then becomes an impenetrable prison that shuts out living concern from the one who lies in its depths. It is evident therefore that not all silence is beneficent, and that some silences are malign in their psychic content. It is from the pain of such negative silences that most of us flinch, for a long-continued silence of this type can make living alone, even for a brief period, a fearsome experience. Indeed, the prospect of several days' imposed silence is enough to deter most of us from making a retreat. In this respect men are generally more afraid than are women. As we have already noted, men tend to gravitate further away from their centre than do women. They are polarized between the seductive realms of material achievement and intellectual attainment and to have to quit these havens of inner safety for even a few days in order to explore deeper planes of reality is a threatening prospect. In my experience, however, once a person has been properly conducted into the silence of a retreat he is loath to return to the shallow, jarring conviviality of the outer world, for he has glimpsed something of his eternal home in the depth of eternity. Again, the success of this enterprise depends on whether the retreatant has discovered and explored the secret place within, and the responsibility for this depends not only on his own willingness to be led by the Holy Spirit but also on the openness of all those sharing the retreat with him. The catalyst is the conductor, who has to leave self behind and be the instrument

27

of the Spirit of God. This is something that is learned from the experience of life rather than acquired from another person's teaching. And the seal of all authentic retreat conductors is the many days they have been obliged to live alone, like Jesus, in the wilderness and be tested by the devil, who reveals himself as the tempter of good things provided one bows down and worships him. This, in effect, means that one should quit the darkness of silence and seek the idols of the world: wealth, power and the esteem of one's fellows. But the one who persists in the darkness of silence will see the face of God that shines with an eternal, uncreated light of such intensity that all other light is obliterated by its radiance.

I suspect that before we can know the silence of eternity, we have to experience the various unpleasant modalities of silence to which I have already alluded. In the same way we can seldom know God as light until we have penetrated the darkness that seems to surround him. This darkness is, in effect, a psychic emanation of perverted free will, and it arises from the creatures of God who have abused and distorted the creation according to their selfishness and ignorance. The pain of silence is, in one way or another, due to the fear that surrounds it. The basic fear is one of annihilation: if we cannot communicate with other people because we are entirely alone, we fear we will become increasingly forgotten until we cease to register in the minds of anyone. We will then disappear from the light of the living and enter the anonymous darkness of oblivion. This is an ever-present threat that lies on the horizon of a life spent alone. We were never meant to be alone in that terrible dereliction; we were meant to live in fellowship and life, not in cold isolation. It is this fear of gradually disappearing from the light of human concern that makes living alone a forbidding prospect. The silence that envelops one brings with it apathy, exclusion and gradual attrition that ends in death and disintegration.

Not all the fear of silence is due simply to a gradual loss of one's place among the living members of one's society. To it are added the more menacing elements of ostracism and disapproval. The silence that follows society's rejection of an erring member is a fearsome ordeal to undergo. It does not only mean that one is now left completely on one's own. This would be unpleasant enough, but to this enforced seclusion there is added the threat of punishment and destruction. This has been the sequence of events in the lives of the victims of the prison camps in various totalitarian regimes in our own century: first one is ignored as if one did not exist, and then the ruthless destructive power of hatred seeks to annihilate the person completely. In the more circumscribed cruelty of local groups a vicious type of ostracism serves to isolate the unfortunate victim of discrimination, so that few people will dare to have anything to do with him. The terrible aspect of this silence is that it is devoid of any communication – one is completely alone, almost as if the Spirit of God himself is withheld from the one who gropes in absolute isolation.

To be a forgotten person is a terrible thought; it is one of the fears that may beset anyone confronting death. To exist in a vacuum devoid of any human contact is as near an experience of hell as we can bear to contemplate. It is far more terrible in its implications than the traditional picture of hell as a place of physical and mental torture. These tortures, however dreadful they may be, have at least a positive content in that the person's identity is still acknowledged. In the void of oblivion he enters into non-existence, at least in the minds of his fellows, while he remains painfully aware of his continued suffering. The malign aspect of silence thus can be seen as that which denies the person's sense of identity and significance until he enters the darkness of despair, that perverted 'cloud of unknowing' which does not lead to God but to self-abandonment in chaos and destruction.

Well does the Psalmist advise us not to put our trust even in princes. All unredeemed human beings have their price, and then they will betray us. This hard approach to the superficiality of human solidarity has its one saving clause; not all human beings are unredeemed. The ones who have been redeemed are those who have emerged transformed from the pit of suffering so that they function no longer from the consciousness of the superficially placed ego, but from the inner centre of the soul. The ego makes demands for itself, and soon dissociates itself from all relationships that appear to be without profit for itself. The broken, the derelict, and those who are isolated from the world soon cease to

matter in the eyes of the worldly-wise, and the ego dismisses
them from its concern. The soul, on the other hand, is in
constant communion with all life through the shared spirit
within it. It cannot remain impervious to the dereliction and
suffering of any creature, as it is involved in all life. Only as
we function from the depth of the inner place of the soul can
we know the redemption of the world effected by the ministry
of Jesus. Before this change occurs in our own consciousness
the redemption wrought by Christ remains a purely
intellectual concept, a fiction of theological argument. It has
little weight or content in the course of our lives. St John
speaks truly when he says that we know we have passed
from death to life because we love our brothers (1 John 3.14).
This love is, in effect, an awakening of the soul to the love of
God, which then radiates to all life as caring and self-giving.
Furthermore, it is universal in its intensity; it flows out to
those far off as greatly as to those close at hand, and it does
not distinguish enemy from friend. Just as God pours down
his blessings on the just and the unjust alike, so does the love
of the redeemed person flow out as an unquenchable stream
on all who will receive it.

We have, if we are to become fully developed people, to
traverse the dark silence of fear that presages destruction and
annihilation before we can know the other side of that silence
which is the eternal presence of God. What we must be
prepared to surrender even to total annihilation is our sense
of self-importance. We have to be divested of the illusion of
all identification with success and the good things of life. In
other words, the ego has to be brought to the altar for
sacrifice in exactly the same way as Abram brought his
beloved son Isaac to the altar to be given as an offering to
God. It is the ego that fears its destruction, and until that fear
is finally confronted in clear consciousness and unrestrained
self-offering, there can be no freedom from death and
annihilation. We know that, when Abram was on the point of
slaying his son, God intervened and saved the precious
offspring of the great patriarch. Only then was his name
changed to Abraham, which means, on a higher level of
reality, that his nature was changed so that the life of
immortality was brought more clearly within his grasp. By
being prepared to sacrifice his son to God, Abraham had

touched a relationship with Isaac that transcended even the death of the body, and when Isaac was restored, his communion with his father was established to the point at which death itself was merely an incident in immortal life.

It is thus also with the ego. In itself it is a precious aspect of the personality, for it is our means of self-manifestation in the world. Without it we would be insubstantial ghosts rather than living people. But it has a limited currency in its own right; only when it serves as an instrument of the deeper nature is it transformed from a petulant tyrant that demands everything for itself to a gracious servant of the whole person, whose joy consists in participating in the fullness of the life of God as one of many brothers, of giving ceaselessly of itself for the benefit of the whole creation. If one seeks oneself and one's life, one loses it, but when one is prepared to give up everything for God, one knows him and the life that is real. That which was given up is returned renewed and healed; it is redeemed from its end in death to the glory of eternal creation. This is the mystery of eternal life; death is the agent of transformation. When we enter the portals of death, we at last understand that they are also the gates of eternity. The person who knows this is indeed redeemed, for God speaks directly through him, inasmuch as the life he lives is the life Christ lives in him, and all he has is now transformed into Christ (Gal. 2.19).

We can in fact put our trust in no one except God; to know him is the meaning as well as the end of all life. He is not merely a refuge from the storms of life, or a support against intolerable loneliness. He is the basis of everything, the supreme reality, the full relationship by which we know ourselves and other people. The living silence is the way of moving beyond the darkness of the mind's fear of annihilation to the fullness of God's eternal presence.

The darkness of silence has to be penetrated before its final sequence, the passage of the soul to God, is traversed. The true 'cloud of unknowing' is the mystic's negative way to divine knowledge. As one enters this cloud, so all images are divested from one. One property alone remains, the power of love. We are not even aware of any love in the dark silence of self-abandonment; all we know is that we must persist, persevere and continue the journey onwards, which is also the journey inwards towards the soul. It is the love of God that moves us in dark faith onwards towards the unknown goal which is, paradoxically, also the supreme knowledge within us. But what is dimly visible has to be explored, acknowledged and claimed for oneself and for the world. In one of the Parables of the Kingdom, Jesus compares the Kingdom of God to treasure lying buried in a field. When it is found, it has to be put on one side again until the person has acquired sufficient resources to purchase the entire field (Matt. 13.44). The treasure cannot be claimed without the field in which it lies buried.

The first use of silence is therefore to explore the depths of our own personality, to come to terms with the fears and inhibitions that lie deeply placed in the unconscious part of the mind. Inasmuch as the microcosm of the mind of each individual mirrors the macrocosm of the mind of mankind, so the journey inwards is also a participation in the pain, dread, hopes and despair of all people. When Jesus underwent the supreme test of the agony in the Garden of Gethsemane and the subsequent crucifixion, there was no aspect of human dread and dereliction, pain and despair, that he did not touch. It is in this way that he is with all of us in our own agony even though he did not experience the actual modes of torture or distress that came into common use long after his own life had ended. The history of each person may be unique, but the emotional turmoil that underlies it is shared in common by all his fellows. The person who lives alone in silence will have a sharp light of clarity shed on the most intimate and excruciating details of his past life. What starts by being almost unbearable soon assumes the quality of an agent of cleansing, and suddenly one realizes that one is free. The things of the past with their intense emotional charge have at last been seen in their proper perspective, and one has transcended the pain and the indignation that they had previously evinced. There is no authentic spirituality that has not come to terms with the most harrowing details of the world's past in one's own psyche—remembering that the microcosm is a mirror of the macrocosm—and has learnt to accept all in the spirit of love.

When the exploration of the depths of the personality can be tolerated, the silence ceases to be menacing. It becomes

refreshing and comforting, so much so that the circumstances
that caused one to live alone are now seen to be no small
blessing. One can at last learn how to bequeath the blessing
of peace to other people. This is most important, for silence
enjoyed alone can lead to a selfish disregard for other people.
If, however, one has traversed the deep places of the soul, one
undergoes an inner baptism leading to a transformation of
the personality. This inner baptism is a journey from
crucifixion to resurrection, and its fruit is a changed person.
The essential quality of this change is that the person is now
attuned to whatever circumstance assails him. In other words,
he is in the closest union with whatever befalls him or with
whomsoever he may come into relationship. The barrier of
the ego with its suspicion, demands and arrogance is now put
down and a living fellowship is established with each person
in the vicinity or with the situation at hand. Love flows
spontaneously; it is not contrived or forced, but issues forth
from the one to the other. Since all love comes from God, this
means that one is completely open to God whose love shines
on all creation like the rays of the sun. But whereas most of
us have clouds of fear and discontent around us that separate
us from the love of God, the person who is free can absorb
that love and reflect it on to the whole world. This is a great
gift of silence borne in courage and persistence; the soul
becomes purified, even as the soul of Mary was radiantly
innocent to bear the full impress of the Holy Spirit at the time
of the conception of her son Jesus.

The second use of silence is to be able to listen to what
other people are actually saying to us. In what passes so often
for conversation, the speaker is directing a monologue at his
audience, and is interested only in his own ideas and
speculations. His audience is a captive one whose function is
simply to support him, or on whom he can direct his thoughts
in order to see whether or not these are favourably received.
The loquacious person is often in dialogue with himself—the
ego addressing itself—and the audience is hardly given
recognition as a being in its own right. When we are silent
within we can, perhaps for the first time, begin to perceive
the message of another person and listen to him with attention
and concern. This message is something more than a barrage
of words; it is also his inner disposition and the psychic

emanation that arises from it. To read between the lines of another person's thoughts is often as important as concentrating on the articulated word. This is what the deeper listening that comes in silence effects; it is a relationship between people that passes beyond the temptations of judgement, analysis and other worldly wisdom and enters into a union of soul consciousness in which the many are one. The bond of union of souls in the silence of receptivity is the Holy Spirit whose action is no longer distorted by the clamour and the desire for attention of the ego and the reasoning mind. In the tranquillity of a mind freed from the turmoil of personal desire, the message of the cosmos rings in purity and exact formulation. To listen is to be able to receive without judgement, fear or any other kind of inner response the message from beyond oneself. It may come from the heart of another human being, or from the corporate society around one, or it may proceed from the world of the spirit far beyond our mortal comprehension. To listen is the way to all wisdom: the fear of the Lord is indeed the beginning of wisdom and to turn from evil is understanding (Job 28.28). In the watchword of the Jewish faith it is constantly repeated, 'Hear, O Israel, the Lord our God is one Lord' (Deut. 6.4). We cannot hear until we listen; we can certainly hear with the ear whether we wish to or not, but to hear with the mind means taking in the message, receiving it and listening to what it tells us. We know God by receiving him into the soul, and we know other people by accepting them in the everlasting arms of God within ourselves. This is the precious gift of silence.

When we are sufficiently humble of self-regard to take another person, with all his trouble and affliction, into our own being, then we can begin to minister healing to that person. The Holy Spirit, who is the counsellor and the bringer of all truth, enters into the dialogue. He fills us, in ourselves destitute of all understanding, with the eternal wisdom of God, and some of this wisdom can now fall from even the most unlearned lips to lighten the burden of an afflicted brother. Real wisdom is a compound of the knowledge of God working through the chastened soul of a person who has been through the testing-ground of silence long endured and a mind that has learnt keenly in the school of life.

The third use of silence is to listen to what our lives are

telling us about ourselves, to hear the voice of the Holy Spirit leading us into the truth of our condition. As we become quiet, so we can see spread before our understanding the pattern of our past life and the tendencies of behaviour that lie ahead of us. We begin to see how responsible we ourselves have been for the disappointments and failures of the past, and how the weaknesses of character are the truly subversive agent in our lives. We believe that misfortune has led us from one evil circumstance to another, from one unsatisfactory personal relationship to something equally unpleasant. In the silence of inner regard we are shown how culpable we ourselves have been for our difficulties and disasters, what part we have played in the apparently relentlessly inevitable course of our life. A period of recollection is a good discipline of silence at the closing of each day shortly before we retire to a night's sleep. It brings vividly into focus the ambivalence of our attitudes towards other people, how insensitive we are to the suffering of those around us—indeed the part we have played, albeit unwittingly, in adding to another's pain—and how selfish we are in our relationships with those around us. In a retreat the Holy Spirit comes to us in the silence of spiritual effacement and shows us, quite directly, the poverty of the spiritual currency on which we trade. This comes to us in shafts of painful memory and also in a more disguised form as the symbols of a dream. What starts as a painful period of self-examination proceeds with the fascinating unravelling of an inner life story to an experience of unwonted freedom. The promise of Jesus, 'You shall know the truth, and the truth will set you free' (John 8.32), is fulfilled in the life of silence. The truth is that all things, no matter how adverse they may appear to our naked gaze, have a potential to good for those who love God, the source of our being, as St Paul saw so clearly (Rom. 8.28).

The end of silence is to rest in God, in whom alone is one's sustenance and life. To be still and know that God is in command of the world (Ps. 46.10), that indeed he is the only reality, and that he is close to us when we are close to ourselves in the silence of self-giving to the world, is the greatest knowledge we can have. This silence is the precursor of prayer, the dialogue between the human soul and God. We are told to pray without ceasing (1 Thess. 5.18), which means that our attention must always be focused on God no matter what we are doing. If we remember him at all times, no matter where we are or what work we are engaged in, our life will be dedicated to his service and our works will be infused with his spirit. Silence is much more than simply a condition in which there is no speech or noise of any kind. This is the negative aspect of silence. But silence in its greater, more positive dimension, is a condition of attachment of the person to God. One can be silent in the heart of a shattering discourse if one remembers God transcending all distinctions and entering the heart of all that is real. Indeed those intense conversations that proceed to a discovery of the true person lying concealed behind the façade that one puts up against the world are conducted in complete inner silence. The heart of the sacrament of the present moment is the silence in which it is consecrated. Silence is the action of giving up oneself to God, whether in the practice of prayer or in serving one's brother in the world. When one has lost concern for oneself, when one has transcended the barrier that lies between the subject and the object of any encounter, one has entered the silence of eternity. In this silence is the power for any undertaking, because the Holy Spirit inspires the person with wisdom and vision.

The benefits of silence are especially available to the person who lives alone, for he has no one around him to dissipate the stillness. This does not mean that silence should separate one from one's fellows in a vacuum of selfish indulgence. It means that living alone provides an invaluable opportunity for coming to the one thing needful for salvation, the presence of God in the moment in hand. And when we know that presence, we are enabled to take it out with us into the world. The silence of eternity, far from excluding us from the life of the world, is the way in which we can come in full comand of our gifts to the world. Silence in God brings all life to us. It is the only way in which loneliness is effectively banished, for it brings us as whole people to the world. We no longer need the world for support; instead we serve the world as a support through God who works his way in us. It therefore follows that the greatest use of silence is prayer for the whole world, the precious practice of intercession.

FIVE

Living in Abundance

The life alone is not necessarily one of isolation from the good things of the world. It need not be a life apart from other people, a separation due to feelings of inferiority, fear or distaste. It can be a life dedicated to the service of man and the development of the individual to the peak of his excellence. In that excellence he can both commune with God and be the servant of God in the world. I do not believe we undergo any experience merely through blind chance; the apparently fortuitous circumstances of life are here as our testing ground for further development of the personality. Some people need isolation in order to grow into authenticity, that they may be less dependent on the whims and fashions of the society around them. A period in the wilderness, if it serves no other purpose, does at least help one to get one's priorities in order. The things once assumed to be essential for one's life, such as the constant company of other people, society's approval, one's own reputation amongst those who amount to something in the world's eyes, and the number of important people one knows seem suddenly to dissolve like a mist of unreality. It is a revelation in those narrowed circumstances how simple life can be when it is shriven of the accretions of social usage and conformity. What at first seems to be almost too unbearable to confront suddenly widens out into a prospect of inner freedom, perhaps the first opportunity to be oneself since one came to self-awareness when one was a small child. It is at this point that one may begin to know oneself for the first time in one's life. The self one knows is, in fact, a central point within, the secret place which is the cornerstone on which the whole edifice of the person is erected.

To live life in its fullness in the way that Jesus came to fulfil life (John 10.10) is to be fully oneself and to flow out to every circumstance and event in one's life with expectancy and joy.

The full life is not one that need be filled with extraordinary events so that a person is constantly entertained, so that boredom is crowded out by spectacular encounters and the gaping void of inner futility is deceptively carpeted over by the never-ceasing diversions of the moment. This is in reality a way of escaping from life's full thrust, a way of evading the stark, pressing questions of meaning and destiny that lie behind the diverting façade of the present show. The full life is one in which the person is completely open to the present moment, and far from awaiting distractions to mitigate inner inadequacy, gives of himself to that moment. The life of abundance is therefore not so much one in which a person is being continually filled with pleasant things that take him away from his own centre, as one in which the centre is in the closest union with the present moment. This is the inner experience of something that Jesus demonstrated during the whole of his life among us: 'I and the Father are one' (John 10.30). When the life one leads is inseparable from one's deepest consciousness, one ceases to be lonely and depressed; instead, one is relating purposefully to life in whatever circumstances one finds oneself. It is then that the need for diversions, hobbies, even holidays and friendships fades away, for one finds all of these in one and around one at all times. I do not suggest that the person who lives the full life is above personal relationships; far from it, that person is in such deep, indeed perfect, relationship with all things that every part of creation is a friend of his and every work he does is to the glory of God and the benefit of his fellows. In the words of St Paul: 'The life I live is no longer my life, but the life that Christ lives in me' (Gal. 2.19). When we need people around us, we find a lack that cannot easily be filled. Many so-called friends, who form the bulk of most worldly relationships, flinch from their brother who is in pain and distress, because he threatens them with a burden of caring and commitment that they feel unable to sustain. But when we are full of life that springs eternally from the depth of our being, all those around us are revitalized and renewed by our presence, and we are in communion with all life. The fullness of life that comes to the one who is open to all that the present moment can give is like the living water spoken of by Jesus to the Samaritan woman; it will turn into a spring inside that person, welling up for eternal life (John 4.14).

How can one find the life in abundance in which one is so filled with the Spirit of God that one is in eternal communion with all created things? Again this quest comprises two reciprocal actions: the prior grace of God that is always present though seldom acknowledged, and the openness of man. We may be assured of God's grace and presence because of his nature, which is love. But love, though freely available, cannot be demanded or grasped. It can only be welcomed. The inherent courtesy of God is such that he does not force himself on his creatures. If he were to do this, he would, at least to some extent, annul the freedom of choice which is the basis of the free will that he has given them. He stands at the door of the soul and knocks patiently for admittance to what is his own domain, but from which he has excluded himself as a sharing guest until he is bidden to enter. Thus the sovereignty of the human soul is acknowledged. We, in return, are bound to respect the presence of God, to treat him with a like courtesy. If he is grasped, he recedes from us, and we find only a shadow of his presence with us. There is one positive action alone that the will can take in the soul's communion with God: open acceptance, the full nature of which is worship. This is the free giving up of the self to God, and the essential act is contemplation. When one gives of oneself in heart, and soul, and mind and strength to God, all that is in one and of one is now also in God, and the two are one. Then one is filled with the divine essence, and the life one lives is no longer private and isolated but is indeed the life that Christ lives in one.

It is not easy to contemplate God whom no man has seen. The natural mystic comes closest to this ideal of contemplation, since by an inscrutable gift of God, he is aware of the divine presence in his soul and in the world around him. But even the mystic recognizes the enormous expanse of spiritual light that separates the creature from the Creator. St John reminds us (1 John 4.19—20): 'If a man says "I love God" while hating his brother, he is a liar. If he does not love the brother whom he has seen, it cannot be that he loves God whom he has not seen.' In terms of the contemplation that forms the way to union with God, this means that we must start by giving up ourselves in devotion to the things in hand at the present moment, for in even the smallest of them God shows his eternal presence by the love he bestows on all his creatures.

To contemplate the things that confront us minute by minute in the day's work means being aware of them, giving our attention to them and flowing out in recognition to them. It means being grateful that they are themselves however humble may be their form and function. And this gratitude should embrace three aspects: the One by whom all things are created, the creature itself, and the inner gift of being able to respond with a healthy body and an alert mind to the many wonderful things one meets day by day in an on-going life. Jesus tells us quite starkly that unless we become as little children we cannot enter the Kingdom of Heaven; we must accept the Kingdom of God like a child (Mark 10.15). The little child is not conspicuous for its spirituality in terms of such qualities of excellence as charity, wisdom, selflessness or devotion to God: all these have to be learnt and acquired in the school of life. Nevertheless, the child does have the one thing that is needed for salvation, an open mind uncluttered with dogmatism, arrogance and cynicism. Being innocent of subversive thoughts, the child's mind is immediately receptive to the wonders of the present moment. Everything around it still possesses an aura of exquisite uniqueness to the little child; it is seen as a new creation. If we, of adult stature, are to move towards the heavenly Kingdom, we must learn to relinquish our customary attitude of bored indifference to the things around us. Our senses have to be cleansed of the heavy weariness that comes from a long, heedless association with the articles of common life that we have for so long taken for granted and used without reverence. Even an object of great beauty soon cloys if we experience it simply as an article to be used, something apart from us that can be dismissed at will. Only when we enter into its excellence so that it takes its place in the greater vision of reality does it become a testimony to the everlasting providence of God. Its significance transcends its span of temporal existence inasmuch as all earthly things have their day and then perish. On the other hand, that which is acknowledged as a part of divine reality is seen in its eternal form. As such it is cherished in the memory long after its physical manifestation has disappeared in the sands of time. This memory is not merely personal to the one who acknowledged some action or work that excelled in nobility or beauty, and was thereafter changed by its impact. The memory is also part of the psychic life of creation, and is the possession of all mankind; it may be tapped by those who follow on in later generations. Their imagination may then be stirred by a renewed ideal of perfection that leads to the unclouded vision of God.

When we return to the primal receptivity of a little child, every encounter is invested with new possibilities; the amazing things of the world are seen also to be the simplest. We see that God is eternally making all things new (Rev. 21.5). This is not only a prophetic glimpse of the ultimate transformation of the world but also a proclamation of the never-ceasing renewal of nature by the love of God. In this way each moment has its unique validity—quite unlike the one that preceded it—for the person who is aware and actually participating in the life of that moment. The wonder of the world lies in its warm constancy so that we can take each moment as it comes with confidence and expectancy. The child's vision rests on the constancy of God's eternal providence, while it waits in eager expectation for some new thing that proclaims the unfolding of God's purpose in the world. We are allowed to glimpse, by a shaft of deeper knowledge that sustains a firm faith, that his purpose is the raising up of all life to immortality, the resurrection through death to eternal fellowship of all created things.

Contemplating the present scene comprises two reciprocal actions: attention and blessing. The way of attention is that of being aware of the matter in hand; it is receptive and welcoming. The way of blessing is that of giving oneself as a living sacrifice to the world around one. It means first of all a joyous acclamation of the world and then an offering of oneself in its service. When one blesses something, one pours out one's inner essence in love and prayer on to it, with the hope that something of God may rest on it and transform it. The act of blessing is not so much an outer ritual as an inner attitude; indeed, if it becomes an obligatory performance that has to be bestowed on everything and everyone, it soon

assumes the proportions of an intolerable burden. To bless
means to articulate good will to all whom one meets in the
course of a day's work. As soon as one is imbued with the
spirit of good will so that one flows out from the depths of
one's being to another person, one enters into the psychic life
of that person. One begins to know him with increasing
intimacy, not as one to be analysed and manipulated, but as a
brother whom it is one's privilege to know and to help. In
other words, the blessing that comes from God brings with it
a deeper fellowship of souls in which all are one in the power
of the Holy Spirit, who leads us all into the truth of the
situation and illuminates the way of progress to full
humanity.

Good will is the beginning of a changed attitude to one's
fellow men and to the world. It shows itself initially as the
capacity to respond in blessing to a creature, be it a plant,
animal or human being. But the blessing must not remain
simply an inner attitude of benevolence. It must be realized in
actions that have their end in healing the injured and binding
up the broken-hearted. This means that good will has, if it is
authentic and not merely a complacent attitude devoid of
commitment to those in need, to embrace a positive will to
good. This shows itself in giving up one's time and leisure for
the benefit of all who are in difficulties, especially those in
psychic and spiritual distress. This consideration provides a
point of departure in the life of anyone who is obliged by
circumstances to live alone. What might easily become a
solitary, isolated existence if allowed to pursue its own course
can be resurrected into a life devoted to others. Jesus is
sometimes described as the man for others; the one who lives
alone in awareness and contemplation will soon know his
vocation in the ministry of healing and reconciliation. Living
alone provides an admirable means of being available to
many people in need. But I would emphasize that this
availability is the fruit of a long, bitter, exhaustive encounter
with one's inner nature and a slow working-out of personal
difficulties and inadequacies. The end is an emergence from
the depths of dereliction with the scars of suffering as a
testimony that one has fought the great battle with the dark
forces within one and has come through triumphant and
strengthened. If one simply offers oneself to others in order to

evade the challenge of the inner silence that is the entrance to
the truth about oneself, one will use people rather than help
them. The encounter will degenerate into gossip and mischief-
making, a perennial hazard of those who live alone, since
they have fewer family interests to occupy their time and
attention.

The way of gossip can be seen as the antithesis of the life in
abundance. It is a means of escaping from the pressing
demands of life into a secluded realm where one can look
down on other people and dissect their weaknesses with the
destructive zest and shallow morality that arises from malice
and jealousy. There are few more pleasurable diversions for
those who are dissatisfied and unhappy than to be able to
reduce other people to their level of unfulfilment also. It is a
source of relief to most of us to know that our heroes too have
feet of clay, that even the acknowledged masters of the
spiritual life can be cut down to size when we are given inside
information about their private lives. The harm this attitude
effects does not hurt the desecrated victim nearly so much as
the one who has cast the stone at him. The tendency to
gossip, which moves subtly to vicious mischief-making,
prevents the spiritual growth of the agent of the malicious
rumours. When Jesus lay disgraced in the hands of his
adversaries, even his disciples wanted to have as little to do
with him as possible during the final hours of his mortal life,
while the majority of the populace rejoiced in the humiliation
of yet another acclaimed Messiah. How delighted they were
at his impotence on the cross! If the summit of all human
aspiration proves to be only a flat mediocrity, one too is
exonerated from making any special effort to become a real
person. The end of this view of life is parodied in the advice,
'Let us eat and drink, for tomorrow we die' (1 Cor. 15.32). It
is the logical conclusion of the work of those who aim at
demolishing everything that is noble and inspiring, that by its
witness lifts the common man above the limitation of his own
egoism and gives him a fleeting vision of reality.

It is, of course, possible to invest celebrities and cults with
glamour, and we should be alert to detect and cut away any
false sentiment that may cling to a person or an institution.
The aim here is to raise up that which is true and to heal the
errant or distorted person or society. This can be done

effectively only in the spirit of innocent contemplation that sees clearly, acts decisively and heals with love all that is torn down and stripped of its vanity. The end of this destructive work is the raising up to a new vision of perfection the one who had first to be brought low by a confrontation with the truth about himself. This process of stripping away personal illusions is performed by the Holy Spirit during the course of life; we do not have to act officiously as agents of cleansing for our deluded fellows. If we are still and filled with good will, the Holy Spirit will use us in his work of reclamation. He will do this by putting the appropriate words into our mouths at the right time, and inspiring us to the necessary action when the moment is ripe. If we are open in contemplation, we will never be unresponsive to the Spirit of God, who speaks to us through the spirit within us.

The life of abundance is one of blessing. It gives thanks for the blessings that surround it, and it blesses all the things it meets. We begin to know a thing only when we have moved into its essence by giving thanks to God that it is what it is. And then we begin to know ourselves also. This self-knowledge comprises an initial acquaintance with the elements of our personality, such as the practice of recollection will foster. But then comes the more important aspect of accepting what we have been shown and flowing out to it also in an act of blessing. It is hard to bless an unpleasant trait or a destructive attitude that seems to mar our inner composure and darken our relationships with other people. But until we accept every part of our personality as ourselves, rejecting nothing and holding everything as equally dear, we will be at constant war with aspects of our own nature. The teaching of Jesus that we should love our enemies and pray for those who use us spitefully, and that we should not resist evil applies especially to the things in us that are awry and disturbed. Only when they are brought into the greater community of the self and given their due of recognition can they undergo progressive healing, so that eventually they may play their full part in the work of the person. This is also the way towards a peaceful society, but we are deceiving ourselves if we believe that outer peace can be imposed on those around us while we ourselves are in a state of internal disorder. The life of abundance is not merely restricted to the individual; it flows out to the greater world and brings peace to those who are in turmoil, healing to those who are disordered. The psychic rapport that binds us all together in one body is usually so weak that we tend to live fragmented lives. We are so often in conflict with ourselves that we cannot respond in open receptivity to other people, and what we do emit is disruptive to the harmony of the group to which we belong. This again is the antithesis of the abundant life where all are brought into the larger community by the attitude of blessing that extends to those who are far off no less than to those who are near at hand.

Conflict itself is an important part of growth. Where everything is smooth and harmonious there is often little progress. True harmony flourishes in the reconciliation of conflicts by their synthesis into a new understanding of reality. Where conflict becomes demonic in its effect is in those situations in which the opponents seek to destroy each other. Where, on the other hand, conflicting points of view can be surveyed in detachment, a fresh light can be shed on a confusing situation, and all involved in the dissension may grow in tolerance and understanding. Those who live alone, as they grow into that deeper self-knowledge which is the precious fruit of self-acceptance, can be agents of reconciliation for their fellows who are so obsessed with their own point of view that they are unable to appreciate the validity of other approaches to truth. A life alone can make the many-faceted diamond of truth more apprehensible, in that it induces an attitude of non-attachment to the passing scene of life with its numerous distractions and a greater awareness of the principles that underlie constructive living. If people could view the wood of life as something greater than the trees of individual desires, possessions and power drives, they would move beyond acquisitiveness to an awareness of all that is worth while in the world—its freshness, its beauty, its unceasing variety and its challenge each day to fresh fields of human endeavour. These are beyond price, and are held in common by all who are aware and whose contemplation is vibrant with blessings for every created thing.

The life of abundance does not depend on the outer circumstances nearly so much as the inner disposition of the one who responds with his whole being to the vast pageant of

present events. The abundance streams out from within and
enriches the world; it does not need the continual stimulus of
outer events to renew it. The person who lives from the inner
centre, the secret place within, is one from whom the Holy
Spirit pours in unremitting profusion to fertilize all those
around him—not only his fellow beings but also all life. This
is the inner meaning of the ministry of healing; one does not
have to *do* anything so much as to *be* in continual communion
with that which is, whom we know as God.

It can be summarized therefore that the life in abundance
is the life in God, in whom we live and move and have our
being (Acts 17.28). This life is essentially one of constant
acknowledgement of the divine providence by prayer,
thanksgiving and an identification of oneself with all aspects
of the present scene. To see the world eternally anew requires
a self-giving to every creature one meets, a blessing upon all
who impinge on one as one moves through the varied pageant
of life, moment by moment. Even more essential is to be able
to pour out oneself in concern on all who require one's
attention, never forgetting to thank the Creator that the world
is as it is. This is no hollow complacency appropriate for
those whose lives are prosperous and whose future seems
assured, at least in terms of worldly attainments. It is an
intuitive acknowledgement of the essential goodness of life
and the justice of each situation as it arises, that even when,
on the surface, the event appears disastrous, it is invested
with superhuman possibilities that will show themselves to
us provided we have the courage to persist and the faith to
wait. As St Paul says: 'For I reckon that the sufferings we
now endure bear no comparison with the splendour, as yet
unrevealed, which is in store for us' (Rom. 8.18). The basis of
this hope is not wishful thinking. It is a deep mystical vision
of the world of reality that underlies the insubstantial astral
mist in which we live in everyday consciousness. This mist is
a psychic emanation of desire that arises from the unsatisfied
ego, and its components are boredom, fear, jealousy and
resentment. These are assuaged by the constant distractions
that the world needs for entertaining itself and diverting its
attention from the one thing that is necessary for health—the
spirit of truth. Only when the distractions have been finally
torn away in the pain of loss can the reality of God be clearly

known. Then there is silence, and all who can hear will listen
to the message of truth. The truth alone sets us free, because
it tells us of the day when all will be well as we progress
beyond the limitation of worldly selfishness and enter into
the knowledge of eternity. This is attained by living perfectly
in the moment, and offering ourselves freely as a living
sacrifice for all that presents itself to us at that moment.

SIX

The Spirit of Renunciation

———

The life in abundance is balanced by the spirit of renunciation. The doors of perception are not finally cleared so that we are open to the potentialities of the universe until the dross that is wont to occlude them has been removed. The essence of this dross is the desire we all have for such commodities as worldly possessions, power over other people, psychic assurance about future success, and clinging relationships. This last snare to full openness is especially seductive, because on the surface we all know that personal relationships are the very stuff of life. We were never meant to be alone even when we are obliged to live alone. Nevertheless, as long as our attachment to our fellows is one merely of necessity — so as to escape the experience of solitude — we shall never know personal freedom, neither shall we allow our companions to be free of our desire to keep them in bondage to ourselves. There can be no authentic relationship between people who are bound in ties of mutual dependence, inasmuch as each will alternatively try to please the other until the thraldom becomes unbearable, when a complete break may be inevitable. This is the love — hate relationship that prevents many people from attaining inner maturity; instead of pursuing their own path and seeking their own salvation in diligence, they are bound in emotional servitude to those whom they both admire and fear, whose influence is at once invigorating and stultifying. Only when one has learnt how to let another person go can one begin to love that person, even beyond the limits of this mortal life. Love and freedom are indivisible. One can give of oneself freely to the beloved even to the sacrifice of one's own life only when one is a free agent. Even if one is incarcerated in a foul prison, one can still be free in the secret place of the soul, and from this oasis of liberty one can give of one's essence to those around one in

48

love and to those far away in prayer. In each instance the
Holy Spirit is at work in one.

> For love is strong as death,
> passion cruel as the grave;
>> it blazes up like blazing fire,
>> fiercer than any flame.
> Many waters cannot quench love,
>> no flood can sweep it away;
> if a man were to offer for love
>> the whole wealth of his house,
>> it would be utterly scorned.
>> (Song of Songs 8.6−7)

The love that is celebrated in this passage is the tempestuous
passion between two lovers at the height of their relationship.
And when the ardour cools, a more enduring, tender love
warms their souls so that they can be together in silent
contemplation without the need for any tangible reassurance
of mutual support. To know this love is the consummation of
our life in the world. Its origin and end are the love that God
bestows upon us. Its purpose is to bring all created things
into the furnace of love where their dross is refined and their
essence brought into the divine presence, whose end is
transfiguration.

Those who live alone have a special burden of love to carry:
since they are often free from the demands of a close
relationship with one particular person, they are therefore
especially available to enter into a deep relationship with a
number of very different types of people. When what a
person prized most has been taken from him, he may, perhaps
for the first time in his life, be free to take to himself many
things that he had, in his blind arrogance, dismissed out of
hand. In this way the inner purpose of a life apparently alone
is understood; it is to be a life in the midst of many people
whom one previously would hardly have noticed, let alone
approached, in the spirit of friendship.

Renunciation is seldom undertaken in an attitude of free
will; much more often it is thrust upon one. The things in life
that are valued most are suddenly taken away, and one is left
alone. Misfortune strikes suddenly and with it go all one's
previous illusions about one's security founded on ownership.

In the end our most precious possession is our health — bodily, mental and spiritual — without which all the money in the world is tantalizingly useless to attain true satisfaction. Once our personal integrity has been assured our second priority for happiness is our relationship with other people, notably our family and intimate friends. The bottomless pit that a bereavement may expose is a stark reminder of the vital part that even one person can play in our lives; when he departs, our life lacks meaning, and the springs of our actions dry up. The third requirement for fulfilled living relates to our worldly concerns, notably the work we perform and the material security we enjoy. To live without having work to do is an experience that an increasing number of people are knowing, as the tragedy of unemployment afflicts ever more of the world's population. Even if their material wants are satisfied, their integrity as human beings is undermined when they are denied any useful place in society. The dignity of man is closely related to his function in contributing to the world through service and creativity; once he is prevented from fulfilling any useful role he undergoes an inner disintegration that spells ruin to the personality if it is not rapidly reversed. And yet, as one gets older, even in an affluent society, so the inroads of physical enfeeblement as well as the claims of those younger than oneself make retirement from work a social as well as a personal necessity.

When one is faced with the fact of loss and the inevitability of renunciation, it is important to accept the situation without constantly looking back in regret to the past. A new way of life has dawned, and one must move with decisiveness into the future. The secret is, as has already been made clear, to live in the moment and to let the menacing loneliness of the future take care of itself. As one progresses in the testing school of life, so one begins to realize that one is not entirely responsible for one's own existence; admittedly the responsibility for one's actions lies heavily on oneself, but there seems to be a vaster plan at work than we, with our limited vision, can understand. Provided we play our part by doing our best minute by minute in the ever-changing flux of life, our more distant needs seem to be provided for in ways that are beyond our comprehension. It is this mysterious fact of life that we acknowledge intuitively when we believe that all will be well in the end provided we do our best and trust in God.

This trust in God is something more than a passive belief that God will intervene on our behalf to make all things safe and prosperous for us. Such an attitude has a childish irresponsibility about it that could lead to disaster. To trust God means praying without ceasing, remembering him not only during the times set aside for prayer but also when one is in the heat of life's struggle for survival. To remember God in our work means to do everything to his power and glory, and to see him as the nameless Christ who shows his face in the stranger whom we meet in the street and at the place of work. In what to me is the most evidential, as well as the most sublime, of all the resurrection appearances described in the gospel, the risen Lord appears to a group of disciples walking on the road to Emmaus as a stranger who gradually imparts to them the teachings of eternal life as they offer themselves to him in rapt attention. When they proceed to share a meal with him and he breaks the bread and says the blessing, their inner eyes are opened and they at last see him with whom they have been in conversation as their Lord (Luke 24.13—32). When we give ourselves fully to the moment in hand, God is with us also and our trust in his providence is the height of wisdom. In him alone can we attain peace and do the work for which we were called.

Living fully in the moment in the spirit of God allows us both to do our present task well and to forget the clamant ego with its fears and demands. As soon as we can move into a consciousness above that of self-concern, new possibilities open up for us. As Jesus says: 'No one who sets his hand to the plough and then keeps looking back is fit for the kingdom of God' (Luke 9.62). This is the heart of the matter. Once we set our face to the new situation and confront it boldly and with dedication, the difficulties that seemed insuperable now begin to smooth themselves out so that we can see a way to surmounting them. It is thus that hope enters our heart and gives us the impetus to a fresh initiative in life's present trial so that we may rise to future glory. The spiritual law is that, as we give of ourselves to the present situation, so we are filled with the Holy Spirit and given new insights into the future pattern of our life and new strength to realize it.

There seems an almost clinical detachment in this; I would prefer the concept of non-attachment, a vital part of the spiritual life stressed by all the mystics and emphasized especially in the Buddhist tradition. Detachment has the less acceptable side of non-involvement, of viewing everything from the distance but taking care not to be personally implicated. There is no growth in such an attitude, which is really that of the bystander. Non-attachment means a state of not allowing oneself to be captivated by any object or person, so that one's first allegiance is to the Supreme Being. He is eternally with one though seldom acknowledged, because one is so enslaved to the things around one that one's field of spiritual vision is occluded almost to the point of blindness. When our first allegiance is to God, his love fills us, and we give that love to all around us, whether the people with whom we work or the objects that we cherish. Non-attachment is balanced by commitment, not an hysterical, possessive clinging in which we will not let the other person be himself, but a silent, strong undertaking to be loyal to many people for their good and for the love of God. This is the great lesson that comes from renunciation. Until we let go of the lesser we cannot assume our place of responsibility for the greater.

Perhaps the most poignant renunciation that most of us may have to make follows the departure of a loved one, taken from us by death. Bereavement strips us of a sustaining relationship with a beloved person, so that from henceforth we have to live on our own. There is a considerable difference between the life of a person who has always lived alone, whether through choice or necessity, and the life of one who has long been enclosed in a loving relationship only to be suddenly stripped of it and left on his own. The wrenching apart of an old attachment and the void of loneliness that gapes in front of one can be unbearable if confronted starkly without prior preparation. It is well known that the bereaved person may require at least two years' adjustment before he comes fully to himself again. The removal of a loved companion renders life meaningless, at least for a considerable period, until one has regained one's bearings and begun to see the path ahead. Life that is tolerable must be imbued with purpose to give it meaning. The human mind cannot tolerate meaninglessness, for a meaningless life can assume a quality of non-existence that seems worse than death itself. For death is the great unknown experience which may conceivably open up a new vista of fulfilment, whereas the interminable misery of a mortal life that is purposeless and devoid of growth is something that can scarcely be contemplated in normal consciousness. How can one proceed with living in such circumstances? This is the valley of the shadow of death, cold and featureless, that is mentioned in Psalm 23. Until one knows its contours and extent as well as one does one's native domain, one has not tasted life fully. The end is a changed person, one who lives the transpersonal life, whose perspectives are no longer limited to human objectives but are infused with divine forebodings. One becomes a servant of God and shows this in unremitting self-giving to one's fellows.

It is vital to recognize that the past is behind one, and that life continues until the whole creation is lifted up and transfigured to spiritual radiance. Thus, in relation to bereavement, it is necessary to leave the dead to bury the dead and to continue ever more intensely with living the good life here and now. This leaving the dead alone does not mean forgetting them or never alluding to them directly. Indeed, I am sure our prayers are of great importance in the well-being of those many souls not far progressed on the other side of life. But they should be allowed to seek their own salvation in fear and trembling, and not be constantly pestered by our attempts to communicate directly with them. Clinging to the past is a most effective way of thwarting one's own growth and that of the other person also. It is all too easy to bind our loved ones who have died in an emotional prison where they cannot proceed in the life beyond death; until they are set free from the emotional dependence of their loved ones they cannot grow. Memory of a possessive intensity can prevent the growth of those on to whom it attaches itself. This principle is seen in this world also, when for instance, a parent continues to regard his grown-up children as they were many years previously, helpless infants who had to be cuddled, fed and cleaned. Indeed, the relationship between parents and children will continue to be abrasive until the parents have grown up to the fact that their children are individuals in their own right and not extensions of the parent's personality.

They have their own destiny to fulfil, and one of their functions is to guide their parents into a proper understanding of renunciation. This alone will lead to a fulfilling and loving relationship with them. When we see our role in this life as one of stewardship of all the world's resources, we are coming to a mature understanding of the meaning and purpose of our transient mortal existence. The custody we bestow on the earth's bounty and on those closest to us in relationship is the way to their regeneration and transfiguration.

Of course, the memory of the pleasant times of warm companionship in the past will recur as old associations come to mind: the empty chair by the fire, the place where once a bed was used, the single ticket to the lecture or concert, the photographs that captured a moment of intimate bliss. When these show themselves, the heart seems to recede into the void beneath, and a pang of unassuageable grief bears us down to the hell of silent despair. The ache of a soul that is bereft of its companion is like an unending dirge to which the dark foreboding of the barren future adds its gloom. Sometimes one may really believe one has recovered from one's bereavement, only to be shown in a dream the power of the emotional charge that still persists. One then learns how deeply the wound has penetrated and how far it is from being healed. And indeed it can never be obliterated inasmuch as its trace will always remain even in the radiance of future joy. It is a part of one's experience and is deeply engraved on the soul, as the wounds of Jesus are a perpetual testimony to his presence and a guarantee of his identity, even in his risen form. But now they are objects of worship; in the same way our soul's pain is the only way of entering the pain of all our fellow men through the pain endured by Jesus.

'In truth I tell you, in very truth, the man who does not enter the sheepfold by the door, but climbs in some other way, is nothing but a thief or a robber. The man who enters by the door is the shepherd in charge of the sheep' (John 10.1). The true shepherd, typified by Christ, knows his sheep because he has entered their souls and recognizes their troubles. So it is with the man who has experienced the hell of loss and persevered through the arid valley of bereavement. When he comes to the other side — which is another way of understanding the coming to oneself after the illusions of the past have been stripped away—he is one of many brothers to succour those who remain in agony. And by his selfless renunciation he can draw all who are weary and ill at ease to him in the light of God—'and I shall draw all men to myself, when I am lifted up from the earth' (John 12.32).

In the enforced renunciation of a loved one taken away by death, or of a bodily function permanently ruined through the inroads of disease or by the precipitate blow of an accident, once we have come to terms with something that is irreparable, we are free to enter into the depths of all suffering. No one who is human is any longer foreign to us. 'Enter by the narrow gate. The gate is wide that leads to perdition, and there is plenty of room on the road, and many go that way; but the gate that leads to life is small and the road narrow, and those who find it are few' (Matt. 7.13 — 14). Only those who have been shriven of all conceit, of all illusions of personal ownership, of all vanity based on psychical or intellectual gifts, indeed of all clinging to possessions, can find a place through the small gate on to the narrow road whose destination is the life abundant. This is the crucial lesson of loss; it is the bitter fruit of bereavement which, once tasted, becomes sweet with the promise of universal healing.

When we have lost that which appeared to be essential for our well-being, we can at last rest in him who is. We, as if by a sudden blow of divine understanding, come to recognize the unassailable reality within that endures all outer storms. He is the rock deeply implanted within the soul that is also the rock on whom we lay our weary heads and rest as Jacob did when he had his cosmic dream of angels moving to and from God to his creatures (Gen. 28.10—19). When we know this rest, we do not have to project our thoughts into the unknown, troubled future—troubled through the perversity of man's actions and the dark psychic forces that both determine them and feed off their baneful results. Instead we can live constantly in the present. Only in this way can we contribute constructively to the future, both personal and corporate, so that the peace of God may begin to calm the troubled psychic currents around us and bring relief to the distraught minds of men. When Jesus was about to give up his mortal life on the cross, though filled with doubts about the result—even the validity—of his mission on earth, he rested finally in his

Father, who remained hidden from him during his final trial, and said 'Father, into thy hands I commit my spirit' (Luke 23.46). The mortal mind has ultimately to accept its childlike ignorance about the things of eternity, and to rest in faith on that hiddenness of God (Isa. 45.15) which defies all understanding, before it may pass from death to life, from corruption to transfiguration. We cannot recapture that which has passed beyond the sphere of mortal limitation, but if we are still and give fully of ourselves to the moment in hand, all that was lost will be restored to us, transfigured and entire. This is the authentic way in which our loved ones commune with us in the life beyond death; the initiative is theirs, and what they reveal of themselves is of an order entirely more beautiful than we ever knew of them when they were with us in the flesh.

This is, paradoxically, true also of those who have had to renounce some bodily function, whether sight, hearing or mobility. As long as they fight desperately to retain the power that is waning, so long will they be imprisoned in their impotence while raging with futility against 'the slings and arrows of outrageous fortune'. But once they accept a new life of physical limitation with graciousness and childlike trust, so will new spiritual faculties be revealed in them. In fact, of course, these potentialities were already there but remained dormant, because they were disregarded in the bustle of everyday life, where the things of the spirit amount to little until the powers of this world are revealed in their vanity. This demonstration is brought about by suffering, so that what is real may be exalted and what is illusory undermined, destroyed and resurrected into something of permanent value. An example of this may be the glory an athlete has to yield when he is permanently crippled by a serious accident. His old life is over: all that remains are painful, though precious memories of past contests and triumphs. But if he proceeds with courage into the future, apparently barren of any further use for himself now that his talents are destroyed, he may develop a compassion for others that was previously eclipsed by his own prowess and reputation. This inner spiritual development may be the way in which he devotes the remainder of his life to caring for the crippled and the disowned, so that they may attain a bodily health and proficiency that he was obliged to surrender. The ways of God are indeed strange; his purpose is, however, always the same: to reclaim the lost, to bind up the broken, to heal the sick, and to bring all creatures to the altar of deification, whose great high priest is the resurrected Christ.

In the same way it is uplifting to sense the calm, placid mien of a blind person. His old independence is no longer available, and he trusts entirely on the guidance of those with seeing eyes, including the wonderful companionship of trained dogs who have attained a human fidelity and proficiency through devoted training by those who love animals. And yet as the outer eye fails, so the inner eye of knowledge and love may be opened. When Jesus healed the man born blind, he opened both the outer and the inner eye of this witness to God's glory. Those who contested the blind man's healing, though preserving good outer vision, remained spiritually blind (John 9.1−41). Living alone, by the process of inner revelation, removes the scales from the eyes of the soul, so that one begins to see things that are invisible to those who skim perpetually over the surface of life.

Of all the enforced renunciations that bring people to an experience of aloneness, none is, to my mind, more isolating than that of deafness. Whereas the blind evoke a ready sympathy for their helplessness, so that any aware person will bestir himself to be of assistance as a guide and protector, the deaf tend to bring out the baser qualities in those with whom they try to communicate. Irritation at his apparent inattention, annoyance, ridicule and eventual avoidance is all too often the sequence of events in the life of one who cannot hear his compatriots speak. In addition, he is deprived of the balm of beautiful music that lightens the soul's weary burden. Once again the way forward is to accept the loss, mitigated, of course, as far as possible by the amelioration that modern hearing-aids can provide. When one can rest in one's present situation, new powers of perception are granted one. Thus the blind person's senses of touch and hearing become unusually acute as does the deaf person's sight. Both may be aware of unusual psychic sensitivity also, so that they can discern the atmosphere of a place or the disposition of a group without knowledge about its antecedents. All this occurs especially to those who do not hanker after past ways of life, but proceed instead with faith into a new situation. It is important to face one's defect, whatever its nature, and confide it to those whom one believes are sympathetic and trustworthy. On the other hand, one should be careful not to overwhelm even one's friends and closest associates with constant demands for help, since all people have their breaking-point. It is often those who amount to little in the world's eyes that afford the most loyal support, whereas imposing names only disappoint us by their apathy and coldness. The best way to proceed when deprived of a vital means of communication is to be oneself with courage even in one's deepest destitution. In this way help is more likely to be offered spontaneously, and it can then be accepted in gratitude and with dignity. It is important to bear in mind the principle that he who receives help bestows a priceless gift on the one who has given of himself in help; the transaction is mutual to the end that all who are involved should transcend the tyranny of the egocentric world dominated by rewards and obligations. They should proceed to an experience of the true self which is in communion with all that lives and also with God. The binding force of self-revelation is love.

It is worthy of deep meditation that nothing that lives ever stands still. There are, to my mind, few sadder people than those who try continually to get in touch with their dead through the agency of mediums. Even if the source with which they have made contact has its own identity, even if it is part of the personality of the one who has died — and this is a very questionable assumption — it is still involved in the restricted ego-life of the old unchanged person. It would be sad indeed if after death we continue in essence to live in the same state of self-centred limitation that we knew when we were still alive in the flesh. It is not surprising that those of the departed with whom contact is alleged to have been made on numerous occasions seem to be at the lower end of the spiritual ladder. The advanced soul has far too fine a spiritual radiance to be able to tolerate the coarse vibrations of a human intermediary; on the other hand, it can make its presence felt directly in the mind of the one it loves with such penetration and power that the beloved knows with a certainty transcending rational proof that life continues beyond death. This communication has mystical overtones inasmuch as it lifts the bereaved person far beyond the prison of past memories and present anguish to a realm of pure bliss, where the Godhead pours out love eternally in a world of fathomless unity.

We gradually learn that the physical senses of sight, hearing, touch, smell and taste have their inner subtle counterparts that emanate from the true self. Though our outer humanity may be in decay, yet day by day we are renewed inwardly (2 Cor. 4.16). It seems that in the loss of physical attributes that follows illness and the process of ageing, those of us who are spiritually attuned are given proof of deeper, more enduring spiritual gifts. When we die these spiritual qualities should be so well developed that, deprived as we then are of all physical means of communication, we can commune with each other and with God directly through the portals of the soul.

Thus the tribulations of this life that culminate in the agony of renunciation bear their fruit in the form of a personality so cleansed and purified that it can be an effective instrument of God's purpose. It is transformed from an outer edifice of self-centred will to an organ of service for our thoughts, words and actions, to pervade the whole world and for us to be God's instruments in transforming the society in which we live. This cleansed personality forms the basis of the spiritual body that survives death, and traverses the many valleys of suffering, learning and repentance that are encountered in the mansions of God's house, until it emerges in glory where it knows Christ directly. For this process to be complete the person is changed into the likeness of the Lord, for we know that we shall be like him when we see him as he is (1 John 3.2). Indeed, the spiritual body emerges from its lowly physical mould as an organ of extreme sensitivity, chastened and refined by life's vicissitudes and transfigured in the dark wasteland of suffering. Only when it has wrestled manfully with the angel that threatens disintegration, and has prevailed in faith, can it claim its blessing: freedom not only for itself but for all that exists. It works towards this end by loving all things and giving perpetually of itself to them.

SEVEN

The Burden of Sensitivity

It seems, almost by a pre-ordained scheme, that those who are destined to live by themselves for a long time, are unduly sensitive people. This sensitivity has two parts, an extreme responsiveness to the outer currents of the world, and a deep inner vulnerability that makes one flinch with pain at the manifest cruelty of society. This inner vulnerability, however, is not only affected by events outside one; it also registers the deep, recurrently emergent pain that has accrued following past injuries and insults, and is indeed in psychic communion with the thoughts and emotions of all people. This intimate psychic fellowship extends from the living to the dead, so that no created thing is outside its influence. While finer degrees of sensitivity can be seen in various individuals living a communal life of prayer and service, it is in those who are obliged to spend much of their life alone that the impact of pain from deeper sources than the merely physical world impinges most acutely. They have nobody near them on to whom the burden can be deflected, nor a communal social talk that can indefinitely occlude the awareness of deeper sources of unrest and travail.

The first type of sensitivity that is to be encountered when one is alone is the impact of memories of the past on one's present awareness. In the cut and thrust of general conversation these can be summarily dismissed from one's field of consciousness and allowed to become dissipated among the elements of the unconscious. In due course they emerge once more, usually disguised symbolically in our dream life, where once again they are rapidly dismissed from memory until their psychic charge becomes so loaded that they have to be acknowledged in clear consciousness, examined and resolved. This process is accelerated during an effective retreat; it is the Holy Spirit, the one who leads us to all truth such as we can bear at the present time, who reveals

60

our past attitudes, inclinations and dispositions to us, and makes us face up to our responsibilities. We have to assimilate the unpalatable details of our own complicity in the misfortunes that have dogged our lives and the potential harm we have done to others, not only directly but also at a distance by virtue of our lack of charity and our resentment based on jealousy and fear.

Unpleasant as all this is, it can be gradually alleviated as the retreat proceeds and the Holy Spirit continues his work of integrating the lost, and now rediscovered, elements of the psyche, into the full personality. The essence of healing is acceptance. We cannot accept the unpleasant, perverse side of our nature until we have experienced acceptance of ourselves as we now stand. The image I strive to project is the self I would like my friends, and indeed the world, to believe in. Such a personage is artificial, having no intrinsic life in it. Only when I face the full force of my being as I now am, can I rest in myself and give myself wholeheartedly to God. Thus the apparently worthless publican is more acceptable to God than the outwardly worthy Pharisee, in Jesus' most central parable (Luke 18.9 — 14). The sinner, aware of his dereliction, can give only himself to God, and being empty of conceit is in a state of openness to God's grace. By contrast, the conventionally religious man is so full of his own piety and good works that he can hide behind them, effectively giving nothing of himself away at all. Those who believe they have arrived in heaven are farthest from its bounds, especially when their attitude is based on doctrinal rectitude. The ones who are in heaven are those who have lost concern for themselves in their prayer to God and their service to their fellow men.

Living alone has much the same effect of self-exposure that is produced more genially in the atmosphere of a retreat, when one is flanked about by other seekers on the way and is under the tutelage of a conductor who ought to be able to afford relief from the more painful pangs of conscience. In the life apart from others there is often no one to help shoulder the bitter burden of self-revelation that emanates from elements of the unconscious. One can consequently become submerged in the rising waters of past unhappiness so that life becomes unbearable. In this respect it is the early hours of the morning that witness the most powerful surges of emotional pain. When one awakens from a troubled sleep the barely articulate fears that are usually just below the surface of one's consciousness rise in terrifying determination, so that one's whole mind soon becomes a seething mass of confusion, resentment and blurred hatred against those whom one, in this state of troubled thought, feels are taking advantage of one. Sometimes the impulse to do something immediate to relieve the inner tension may become irresistible and in the heat of the moment one may write an abusive letter. The telephone would be another outlet for emotional release, but for the fortunate circumstance that, being so early in the day, it would probably remain unanswered should one unburden oneself on one's sleeping compatriots. And indeed, it is most important to do and say nothing precipitate during such a paroxysm of emotional anguish. If only we could check ourselves during phases of tempestuous anger, the amount of emotional debris we would let loose into the psychic atmosphere would be greatly reduced. A clean psychic environment is a prerequisite for a healthy physical world, one in which the debris of violence and conflict could be kept to a minimum as people learnt to live more peaceably together.

To check one's emotional imbalances does not mean denying them, let alone suppressing them. The ultimate effect of such inner subversion would be a sickly, hypocritical relationship with other people and later, as the whole personality revolted against this dishonesty, psychosomatic disorders which might find their end in serious bodily disease. The important precaution always to take is to unburden oneself alone in the silence of the secret place where God comes to us in prayer. What is confessed to oneself in God's manifest presence is cleansed of malign psychic currents, and is thereby already undergoing the first stages of the process of healing. The same principle applies to the early part of bereavement. While, as I pointed out previously, one must leave the dead to bury their dead as one moves onwards into the present moment with awareness and resolution, it is also important not to suppress one's grief, especially during the first months after the death of a loved one. The first anniversary is a particularly painful period, and the release of pent-up emotions associated with the reawakening of precious memories must not be inhibited. The sacrament of the present moment includes not only the outer events of life that one confronts moment by moment, but also the inner psychic life that impinges itself on one's awareness continually. Beautiful scenery, for instance, not only evokes an intense aesthetic response but may also recall a past rapture with someone who is now dead or perhaps has moved away to another part of the world. The juxtaposition of these two emotional impulses has the effect of lifting one's consciousness to a sublime grasp of reality in which the transience of physical beauty is aligned with the deeper meaning of eternal life. That which is beautiful and noble outlasts its physical form and remains an inspiration to all who subsequently pass on that road of life. When we attend to the present moment and give our life to the passing scene, we add our unique flavour to that moment and that scene so that both the world and ourselves are translated to a new place of bliss. It is in a passing shaft of heightened awareness, such as may follow a sensitive appreciation of the transience of all worldly beauty, that one may be transported to the realm of mystical union and see the eternity that underlies all earthly creation. Then one knows that death is not the end of life but rather its moment of transfiguration to a more spiritual dimension of reality.

The spiritual life is one in which the deep core of inner discontent, to which have been added the various burdens and sorrows of the past, is progressively encountered, explored and transfigured. The journey to God is also the journey deep into one's own psyche: the way up is the way down, and heaven can never be attained until hell is acknowledged and reclaimed. The 'harrowing of hell' that Jesus undertook after the crucifixion was the final work he did on the astral planes before his resurrection. But it is important to note that he was intimately involved in the work of hell from the time of his baptism, when the Holy Spirit descended with unique authority on him and led him out into the wilderness, which we call the world, to be tempted by every dark force in creation. Each temptation has to be met without flinching, acknowledged for what it is and embraced in love. Hell is prayed over that its inhabitants, who are all of us at least for some period of our lives, may be cleansed in love and renewed in purpose. In this way alone is the thing of darkness reclaimed so that it too can attain entry into the realm of light, which is the deeper meaning of heaven. In this light there is physical radiance, mental illumination, emotional unburdening and spiritual transparency. Only that which is explored and accepted can be changed by the power of love. By love alone is the evil brought to the good, death raised up to eternal life.

Therefore one's sensitivity should make one more available to intercept the dark forces that pervade the cosmos. As one enters the spiritual realm of light, so one can accept all pain and evil, acting as an agent of transformation to convert the powerful negative influence of malice and fear into the warm radiance of recognition and blessing. This is the very antithesis of pouring out one's anguish and venom on to everyone in the vicinity. The destructive emotions let loose in this way cause a general upheaval of relationships and set in motion negative feelings of fear and distrust. The importance of our thoughts in affecting not only our own lives but also the psychic environment we share with those around us — and indeed the world — is well recognized by schools of metaphysical speculation that emphasize the power of positive thinking. However, the good effected by this rather naive approach to the problem of misfortune and evil is seldom of a high degree. The reason is that superficially articulated positive thoughts proceed from the ego rather than the depths of the self. It is what comes out of the depths of a person that affects him and those around him. As a man thinks in his heart, so is he (Prov. 23.7). The heart is, in this connection, the deep unconscious layer of the mind where there lie submerged many emotional memories of past unhappiness. It is these thoughts that have to be exposed, relived, and accepted before they can be healed and brought into the wider company of the personality. Only then can positive thinking be undertaken in a spirit of authentic belief. And indeed the end of our spiritual life should be one, not so much of thought as of contemplation, when we, receptive, alert and dedicated, are filled with the Spirit of God. It follows therefore that, in dealing with destructive emotional forces that assail us when we are on our own, there should first of all be a frank acknowledgement of the pain of emotional upheaval. It should then be lifted up to God in rapt contemplation, so that the Holy Spirit may show us the deeper significance the pain has in our lives. After that it is possible to accept the negative emotion in a creative spirit and eventually even to love it for acting as a gateway into the psychic life of the many deprived, underprivileged people in the world. Only then will the Holy Spirit proceed with his great work of healing that which was broken and distorted.

So long as we can contain the pain within us, neither denying its existence nor flinching from it, it will cause no psychic disturbance outside us. And when it is blessed in the name of God, its negative emotional charge is neutralized, as it becomes infused with warmth and love. In St Francis's famous prayer one asks to be made an instrument of God's peace. It is only when peace has been established in one's own inner domain that one can bring peace to the greater world around one. The positive action of peace is blessing every circumstance in one's life in God's name. Then even a potentially destructive attitude may be so transformed that it ceases to threaten the integrity of the personality and starts instead to bring harmony to those in one's vicinity. The deeper internal spring of peace is an intimate relationship with God in which one also enjoys boundless communion with all created things which are now transfigured into their eternal form. This is the peace that the souls of the blessed dead enjoy in the hands of God—an intimacy in which they know him even as they are known. And when I know myself in the light of God's love, I know everyone else also in that light. Then alone do I understand that in obeying the second great commandment—to love my neighbour as myself—I am realizing as well as affirming my identity with my neighbour. In the sight of God we are all one since God loves everything he has created. It is important in this respect that we exclude in our minds nothing from God's love, no matter how evil and destructive it shows itself in our lives. The difference between the good and the evil agent—ranging from the subtlest psychic emanation to the humblest physical form—lies in its receptivity to God's love. While God causes his sun to rise alike on the bad and the good and his rain to fall on the dishonest as well as the honest, it is only the good and the honest that are receptive to God's goodness and capable of bringing what they have received back to him with a blessing. The evil ones dissipate and squander all they receive, and are in the end as deprived as they were in the beginning. But God never ceases to care for them, hoping always that their hearts may change and their dispositions turn to love him and their brethren travelling on the road of life.

But not all unpleasant emotional forces originate from the depths of the personal psyche. To be sure, they all traverse the psyche of the individual as they impress themselves on the conscious mind, but there is a much deeper terrain of shared psychic experience that proceeds from the collective unconscious to assail all those who are especially sensitive to its impulse. The source of these forces may be the accumulated evil that has existed from the time that the creatures of God first acted independently of him and abused the free will that they were given. It may also be a more direct emanation from the mind of another individual still living in the flesh, or else from one in the life beyond death, devoid of a physical body and functioning in a 'subtle' type of body which contains past thoughts and emotions that still await healing and redemption. Such assaults on the psyche of sensitive people who live on their own and have nobody on whom to lean for emotional and moral support may cause acute suffering. This suffering accrues not only from the emotional darkness transmitted from the hidden source to the mind of the lonely recipient, but also from vague, barely assimilated pieces of information that may be laid at the door of his intelligence. It reveals itself in bouts of apparently causeless depression that may on occasion be severe enough to threaten suicide. The type of circumstance that, at least in my experience, is most likely to precipitate such an intense depression is one in which the psyche of a very sensitive person is assailed by the personality of someone whom he knew in the flesh and has since died. The death is often violent in nature, not infrequently with suicidal overtones, and the 'spirit' of the deceased hovers around the psychic aura of the sensitive, isolated person. Not infrequently the sensitive one and the deceased were previously on bad terms, so that the depression involved cannot simply be attributed to grief at the departure of a beloved friend.

In cases of this type there is sometimes an additional history of mental imbalance, and only when the conventional psychiatric and psychotherapeutic measures—which should always be employed first—have failed to help the person does the possibility of psychic obsession, or even possession, present itself to the minds of those concerned in the person's welfare. If the therapist has a psychic gift he may sense the obsessing entity directly. In any case the entity concerned must be delivered from its morbid attachment to the psyche of the sensitive recipient and commanded to seek its place in God's kingdom; on occasions it does not realize that it is dead to the flesh. At the same time the recipient must be instructed to abstain in the future from any psychic practices in which he may have indulged, and instead constantly practise contemplative prayer centred on the presence of God. This type of unpleasant obsession is especially liable to occur in those who dabble in the occult. The work of deliverance, a more constructive term than exorcism since the invading entity must be sent to the place which God has prepared for it and not simply cast into the outer darkness of oblivion, should be performed by an ordained minister in the mainstream Christian tradition, one that has a trinitarian basis, since the deliverance should be carried out in the name of the Holy Trinity. The authority conferred at ordination will bear its own stamp of effectiveness provided the minister accepts it and believes in it, and leads a life befitting one who is privileged to call on the name of Father, Son and Holy Spirit. God alone can deliver us from evil while at the same time caring for the obsessing powers that have lost their way and caused psychic havoc. They too have their share of love in God.

Sometimes the sensitive person is given vague intimations about future events of an unpleasant type, such as accidents that may result in the death of people whom he does not personally know. On occasions he may feel that he should have done something about it, and subsequently be filled with guilt when the event occurs. He may even believe that he was partly responsible for the tragedy. Psychic impressions can wreak havoc on the lives of sensitive people who are ignorant about paranormal phenomena and the tendency of the mind to misinterpret and distort information that it only partially grasps. The situation is not helped by the ignorance and antagonism (the two go hand in hand) shown by most psychiatrists and ministers of religion to the subject of psychic phenomena. It therefore follows that the field is dominated by ill-informed enthusiasts who dabble in occultism and lack proper psychological, theological and spiritual training. The harm that can be done by these practitioners is alarming in its magnitude, since only a psychologically balanced, spiritually experienced and emotionally mature person can have the discernment necessary to interpret psychical communications with authority. The fleeting, nebulous, unpredictable content of psychic information makes it dangerous as a guide to sound living, though on occasion it may shatter the most sceptical mind by its accuracy.

The important principle that the sensitive person should grasp is that God is in charge. He may indeed inspire us with his Spirit to act directly in a confused situation, but he does not rule our lives or trample on our own power of choice. In other words, God strengthens the human will by infusing it with purpose and confidence, but he does not ride roughshod over it. He who stands patiently at the door of the soul and knocks quietly for admission does not take over the personality or control the will. This is the difference between the courtesy of God to his creatures and the power-hungry lust of an intermediate psychic intelligence that uses everything in its vicinity for selfish motives. God raises his creatures to an image of his own nature (as mirrored in Christ), whereas predatory psychic powers reduce all with whom they come into contact to the state of compliant slaves.

To deal with unwanted psychic invasion a determined mind is the first prerequisite. All extraneous influences should be seen for what they are—a foreign interference in the life of a free agent that brings no benefit with it. Even if some of the unsolicited information appears accurate in the short term, it does not contribute ultimately to the welfare of the person, and the end of the matter is a subtle enslavement of the personality and sacrifice of the will to sinister outside forces. The same principle holds true of those who allow their lives to be governed by astrological predictions or the teachings and advice that fall from the lips of mediums. All of these may have enough truth to impress the confidence of those attuned to their utterances, but they do not lead to the full growth of the person. We certainly need to know more about the inner workings of psychic phenomena, for these too are part of God's dispensation. But they are no more acceptable as oracles of truth than are the utterances of the worldly purveyors of wisdom who dominate the fields of politics, economics, psychology or science. The acid test is always the same: by their fruits you will know them (Matt. 7.15 – 20). Spiritual teaching alone affords the word of life, for it brings with it the unconditional love of God and infuses the person with the Holy Spirit who inspires him to new peaks of endeavour in which he himself is the master. Therefore a determined mind will tell all invading psychic influences to depart. The difficulty lies in the ambivalence of most people: they want the best of all worlds. Thus, while they would like to be free of psychic interference so that they can lead an independent existence, they also bask in the unwonted glamour of psychic communication that boosts their ego and promises material benefits. This was the supreme temptation of Jesus in the wilderness, when the devil took him to a very high mountain and showed him all the kingdoms of the world in their glory. 'All these,' he said, 'I will give you, if you will only fall down and do me homage.' The reply of Jesus has to be repeated in the lives of all those who aspire to true freedom, which is God's service: 'Begone, Satan. Scripture says "You shall do homage to the Lord your God and worship him alone" ' (Matt. 4.8 – 10). I would emphasize that it is not the fact of psychic information that is evil, but the source of much of that information. The message of God that lifts up our hearts and sets the captive in us free is also mediated psychically. The discernment of spirits is essential to know the source of the information.

Once the mind has bidden all invading psychic forces to leave its domain, it must seal the door of the soul lest they return, indeed augmented in number, by the invitation of fresh members to the company. Jesus warns us that merely expelling one evil spirit is no guarantee against its later return, indeed accompanied by others even more wicked than itself (Matt. 12.43 – 45). The last state of the person may be worse than the first. The inner chamber of the secret place, where we present ourselves for communion with God, is protected against psychic assault by the practice of prayer. Where God is allowed entry, all subversive powers are, by his very presence, excluded. But it may be necessary to stabilize the psyche against further invasion before prayer becomes possible. It is in this respect that an understanding of the human psychic constitution is of great help.

There seem to be certain bodily areas that correspond to tracks, or channels, through which psychic impulses impinge on the mind, especially that of sensitive people. These psychic centres should be under control so that they do not admit foreign emanations indiscriminately. The centre that is especially important in admitting (or rejecting) psychic material of a strongly emotional charge has its bodily counterpart in the upper part of the abdomen above the navel. If the mind can be fixed on this area of the body while the person is deeply relaxed, a degree of control over the centre can be attained. The way usually recommended is to attend to the rhythm of normal breathing; the abdomen moves outwards with inspiration and retracts during expiration. To make the focus of attention even more definite the sign of the cross can be visualized on that part of the abdomen. If this simple exercise is practised several times each day for about five minutes each time, the psychic centre will come under such control that it will no longer allow the entry of baneful impulses indiscriminately. This exercise is in no way a substitute for prayer, but as I have already mentioned, it may, under some circumstances, be a necessary preliminary action before more profound spiritual devotions can be carried out. Certainly it is hard to meditate effectively until every part of the psyche is at rest to the world and fully attentive to God. When one's prayer life is vigorous, the possibility of obsession by extraneous psychic forces becomes small.

In the end the determining principle is the love of God and the confidence we have that all things work out for good to those who love him. If we can keep our minds fixed on the present moment and all that appertains to it, we will immediately be in psychic rapport with the entire created universe. Then our constant solicitude for the world's problems will bring us into a creative psychic fellowship with our fellows and with all life. We are members of one another at the level of the soul, or true self, and the closer we are to our own souls, the more authentic will be our relationship with all people, and the more immediate will be our knowledge of God. This is the supreme lesson that psychic sensitivity impresses on us. It may be a great burden, but if properly accepted it brings one into fellowship with a vast range of people and lessens the pain of living alone. It is the person who lives alone who will bear the brunt of psychic sensitivity, because there are fewer distractions in his life that would serve to divert his attention to the things of the physical senses. But as he persists in exploring his psychic sensitivity, so new dimensions of spiritual understanding will be revealed to him.

EIGHT

Prayer in Solitude

If, as A. N. Whitehead asserted, religion is what a man does with his solitariness, the view of life that is articulated in our thoughts and aspirations when we are completely alone reveals uncompromisingly our response to the reality of death and the nature of God. 'As a man thinks in his heart, so is he' (Prov. 23.7); it is in the silence of aloneness that the heart's sincere utterance makes itself heard by the whole personality, for then its articulation is the motive force that informs the will and drives the person onwards. Jesus says that where our treasure is, there will be our heart also (Matt. 6.21). The deepest aspiration of the person indicates the seat of his emotional response and the core of his moral nature; the heart in this respect is that aspect of the total personality which responds emotionally to the springs of moral judgement that well up from the depths of the soul and infuse one's life with a meaning that transcends the ephemeral glitter of immediate gratification.

The one treasure that outlasts the changes of the present scene and survives the disillusionment and impoverishment of age is that eternal enlightenment whose source is God. From him alone issues inspiration that never dims, being everlastingly replenished by the power of his Spirit. Our solitariness reveals the true springs of action that energize us; it carries us through the outer distraction of surface life to the ultimate truth. This truth comprises two elements: our own intrinsic nothingness, and the seed of eternal life that lies deeply implanted within us. This seed is the Spirit of God in every man, Christ in us, the hope of a glory to come. Prayer is the way to the knowledge of that glory within which is to change the whole person into something of the stature of a perfect human being, seen in the likeness of Christ. Those of us who live on our own, unburdened by the demands on our time and emotional energy by the presence of others around

72

us—and here I allude especially to the proximity of family commitments that can effectively consume all the time and inner serenity of those on whom constant imposition is made—have a responsibility as well as a heaven-sent opportunity to explore the inner world of the spirit by the action of prayer. It is our duty as well as our privilege to infuse the world around us with the radiance that follows prayer. Only thus can the Stygian darkness that envelops so much human action and understanding be lightened. If the inner eye of spiritual discernment could be cleared, we would at last see the power of God that sustains the world. Then we would begin to work in harmony with the divine presence instead of beating the air blindly in trying to achieve what we, in our ignorance, see as our own best interests. As Psalm 127 reminds us: 'Unless the Lord builds the house, its builders will have toiled in vain. Unless the Lord keeps watch over a city, in vain the watchman stands on guard. In vain you rise up early and go late to rest, toiling for the bread you eat; he supplies the need of those he likes' (verses 1—2). Prayer is our reaching out to God as well as our response to him whereby he and we, working in unity, can build that house which is at once the inner chamber within the soul of each one of us and also the edifice of the world. Prayer is the way in which we stand perpetual watch over the world in the presence of God. It is the communion of the soul with God in which the mind ascends to the divine presence and is filled with good things, even tidings of eternal life.

The prerequisite for prayer is silence. As I have already indicated, silence is mandatory before we can listen to another person speak to us, not only with his voice but, even more significantly, with the whole personality that flows out from him as a psychic emanation. Once we have grasped the message by hearing, seeing and feeling, and integrated it into a composite whole by the combined power of intellect and intuition, we can begin to communicate at a deep level with the other person. In the same way when I am silent before God in contemplation, which is the deepest, most formless, most intense mode of meditation, I can begin to converse spontaneously with him and listen to what he is telling me. We know that silence in the secret place where we are alone to ourselves, where, in the depths of the soul, a communion with God is eternally celebrated. When we are still to the clamour of the world outside and the mind within, when no further noise or images impinge themselves upon us, when distractions cease to hammer on the door of consciousness, a silence descends on us that is a true balm to the soul: it is no negative void but rather the impulse of a positive wave of love that pervades the whole personality and lifts it spiritually to a new revelation of meaning and purpose. This radiation is of God and reminds us of our divine origin and our sacred purpose, which is to return to God with all the material universe that we have lifted up to him in selfless service. That service is consummated in love that God has showered on us, and we, in our turn, give back to him with the impress of our own devotion and sacrifice that charges the love of God with our own dedication.

'Blessed art thou, Lord God of our father Israel, from of old and for ever. Thine, O Lord, is the greatness, the power, the glory, the splendour, and the majesty; for everything in heaven and on earth is thine' (I Chron. 29.10 — 11). Indeed, whatever we choose to give God is his own already, and yet we give him something more whenever we give in thanks and praise. We give ourselves renewed in his love and consecrated by our strengthened wills.

Prayer in solitude starts when the silence of wonder descends on us when, during the sacrament of the present moment, we are lifted above the turmoil of the world around us and see, with supersensual vision, the timeless peace that lies at the centre of the whirl of constant agitation which we call mortal life. This descent of the heavenly silence comes unsolicited as an act of pure grace from God, but, as we grow into spiritual maturity, so we are able to call upon that silence with increasing assurance and be filled with peace whenever the clamour of mundane chaos threatens our composure. We cannot create the silence, which is of God, but we can call upon God in prayer, and his free gift is made immediately available to us. This is, in essence, the way of prayer in solitude: a calling upon the name of God in silence and waiting in calm assurance for his response. This response is a deeper, heavenly peace in which the shattering silence of eternity breaks upon the secret place within and informs it of a meaning beyond articulate formulation. Just as we can

communicate with greater ease with one another when we
know the other better, so we are able to speak to God in the
depths of self-knowledge when we are more open to the
silence of his presence during the course of each moment in
time.

Prayer in solitude is a spontaneous, heartfelt giving of
oneself to God in the silence of the moment. This silence
sustains the vortex of clamour and activity that both
punctuate each moment and shatter its sanctity into frag-
ments of disorder and chaos. But when the silence that lies at
the heart of activity is touched and blessed, the outer activity
ceases to be destructive. Instead it becomes a dedicated act of
the world to God, and everything about it is lifted up from
mortal transience to eternal glory, from death to immortality.
Thus it comes about that the heart of prayer is communion
with God *now*, when we are engaged in our present toil. Then
it can be raised up in dedication to him, and our work too can
find its place in the fabric of the temple on high that is not
made with hands but is part of the eternal abode God has
destined for all his creatures. The plan of the temple of
eternal life is in the mind of God, but the units of its structure
depend on the contribution made by God's creatures. Each
thought plays its part in the eternal world that is our destined
home when we have, in the company of Christ, helped to
raise up that which was mortal to immortality, that which
was chaotic to perfect order.

Thus prayer is a ceaseless dialogue between the soul and
God. Its ground is contemplation, a rapt worship in silence of
God who reveals himself to us as love, and its response is
praise. The praise that issues without restraint from the lips
of the one who prays is a spontaneous acclamation of the
glory of God. In the words of the Gloria, 'Glory be to God on
high and in earth peace, goodwill towards men. We praise
you, we bless you, we worship you, we glorify you, we give
thanks to you for your great glory.' The praise is no fulsome
flattery aimed at pleasing, placating or frankly bribing God,
as is sometimes believed by those who are uninformed about
the spiritual life. It is an uninhibited utterance of joy that
creation is as it is, and its Author, though beyond description,
is nevertheless available to commune personally with the
individual soul. We praise God for himself alone, and for

what he has done in the redemption and sanctification of his creation by the incarnation of Christ and the down-pouring of the Holy Spirit. And then we utter the prayer of thanksgiving for the munificence of God in our own lives. Whereas praise is directed to God alone, thanksgiving brings in our own gratitude for what he has done for us personally. It is a response of the soul to its own healing in God. This constant praise and thanksgiving issues from the aware soul at all seasons of its life. It knows that the sufferings of the present time bear no comparison with the splendour, as yet un-revealed, which is in store for us all (Rom. 8.18), that nothing in death or life, in the realm of spirits or superhuman powers, in the world as it is or the world as it shall be, in the forces of the universe, in heights or depths, indeed nothing in all creation, can separate us from the love of God in Christ Jesus our Lord (Rom. 8.38 – 39).

This is the dialogue of the unburdened soul with God: unceasing acclamation which issues forth in paeans of praise and thanksgiving. When God is the centre of our thoughts, we cease to be alone, and instead become a focus of healing that draws in an ever-mounting procession of people who need spiritual assistance. And once again prayer is the only authentic way in which assistance can be directed to those who are in need, because it is the Holy Spirit in us that directs the work and not our own unaided, arrogant minds.

But what do we actually say to God in our solitude? In fact we say nothing to him until we have heard in hard attention what he has to tell us. It is a well-known insight of the spiritual life that the foundation of prayer is God: Dame Julian of Norwich says that he is the 'ground of our beseeching'. He speaks to our inner self and through that inner self to the mind and emotions, when we are still and open to his discourse. The Holy Spirit speaks eternal truth to us in wordless conversation so that we begin to see the extent of our deficiency, the magnitude of our lack. Truth assails us when we are open to his dissecting logic and inexorable driving power. In the early stages of a person's prayer life this dialogue with God's Spirit, who leads him into all truth such as he can bear at any one time, usually takes place at a moment of desolation. When all outer support has been removed, one is open to the voice, still and small in intensity but uttering a shattering commentary on all one's past life and attitudes, that comes from on high. The futility of so much of our activities, the lack of self-control, the harm we do to those around us by thrusting our emotional burdens on them, the dishonesty of our basic attitudes and the duplicity that punctuates our relationships with other people come clearly into focus. At last we have to confront the truth of our condition: we are the authors of our own present unhappiness, and only a complete change in attitude can effect a change in our outer circumstances. It is salutary to remember that when we acknowledge this insufficiency, this selfish attitude to life, to God, we are not telling him anything he does not know. Jesus reminds us that he knows our needs long before we have put them into articulate formulation (Matt. 6.8), and therefore there is no need to repeat these needs vainly to him so that they may be better heard and acknowledged. Indeed, it is he who is telling us. When we can at last confront our own complicity in the deception of our lives and confess it openly to God, we are in fact telling ourselves in abject humility the extent of our lack of goodness.

In other words, when we make a confession to God, we are asserting in clear consciousness our guilt and inadequacy, so that nothing is kept hidden any longer. Once a frank confession is made, so that the whole personality is involved and the will activated, a change in attitude follows, and this is in due course accompanied by a commensurate change in one's life. The belief in the forgiveness of sins that plays a fundamental part in the Christian insight into the nature of God—and was made historically manifest once and for all in the atoning sacrifice of Christ—depends on our acceptance of God's grace that comes to us without reservation or qualification. Jesus tells us to knock in the full assurance that the door will be opened, to seek in the knowledge that we will find, to ask as an inevitable preliminary for the answer to come to us (Matt. 7.7). But we must play our part in this transaction by asking, seeking and knocking. In terms of the forgiveness of sins this means that when we make our confession we must vow ourselves to spare no effort to lead a new life in the future. The proof that a sin has been forgiven lies in its future disappearance from our lives; when sin is forgiven, we sin no more. One must qualify this radical

statement with the observation that the healing of the
personality is seldom instantaneous, and there may well be
future relapses despite the most sincere intentions of goodness
and selflessness. But each relapse brings with it a more alert
awareness of the fall from grace, a more rapid confession and
a more complete restoration of inner integrity as time goes on.
This gradual journey towards sanctification seems to be right
not only in terms of the slow process of organic growth that
God has ordered for his world and the creatures that inhabit
it, but also because relapses humble us and make us more
compassionate towards our fellow men. Eventually we may
begin to grasp the depth of Jesus' command that we should
not judge or condemn other people (Matt. 7.1−2), for in
doing this we judge and condemn ourselves. We are indeed
all members one of another, and no one can ascend to any
considerable height on the spiritual ladder without taking his
brothers along with him. Our own slow progress is a measure
of the darkness of the world around us, and even if we grow
to a small degree of inner sanctity we are helping to lighten
the burden of those with whom we come into fellowship in
our everyday activities. We attain a greater degree of sanctity
when we carry out our daily duties unselfconsciously and
with concern for other people than when we strive consciously
for holiness. In such an approach to spirituality we resemble
far too closely for comfort the Pharisee, who in Jesus' central
parable was further from a proper relationship with God
than was the despised tax-gatherer (Luke 18.9−14).

A confession to God about our sinful attitudes and actions
leads inevitably to a prayer of petition that the deficiencies in
our character may be healed, and that we may grow in love
and service to our fellow men. Again to ask is to be heard by
God—since he is the source of our petition—but we must
play our part in the transaction. We have already quoted the
opening verse of Psalm 127 to the effect that God is the
source of all building and watching; nevertheless no house is
built on prayer if it remains unconsummated by human
dedication, sweat and toil. Edifices do not materialize from
the heavens; they arise from the earth by the slow labour of
men, who consecrate their souls and bodies to the work of
planning and construction. Faith precedes good works,
inasmuch as works which proceed from the human will

without the prior enlightenment that comes from God are
never totally good. As St Paul reminds us:

> When I want to do the right, only the wrong is within my
> reach. In my inmost self I delight in the law of God, but I
> perceive that there is in my bodily members a different law,
> fighting against the law that my reason approves and
> making me a prisoner under the law that is in my members,
> the law of sin. Miserable creature that I am, who is there to
> rescue me out of this body doomed to death? God alone,
> through Jesus Christ our Lord! Thanks be to God! In a
> word then, I myself, subject to God's law as a rational
> being, am yet, in my unspiritual nature, a slave to the law
> of sin (Rom. 7.21 — 25).

The reason why the law of sin triumphs over our better
nature is because of the recalcitrant quality of the ego; it
believes it has the good of the world at heart when in fact it is
centred in justifying itself and gaining power for itself. Only
when the ego is transfigured by the grace of God does it cease
to do evil and start to do good; it relinquishes its dominant
role in the personality and takes on its proper place as
servant of the Most High, whose abode in us is in the secret
place of the soul.

The proof that God's grace has touched us, that we are at
last in a right relationship with God through faith, is that our
character radiates the warmth of unaffected love and that
works of equal love issue forth from us. As St James says:

> What use is it for a man to say he has faith when he does
> nothing to show it? Can that faith save him? Suppose a
> brother or a sister is in rags with not enough food for the
> day, and one of you says, 'Good luck to you, keep yourselves
> warm, and have plenty to eat', but does nothing to supply
> their bodily needs, what is the good of that? So with faith;
> if it does not lead to action it is in itself a lifeless thing
> (Jas. 2.14 — 17).

He proceeds to point out that faith which is real and not
merely theoretical is proved by the deeds that accompany it.
Thus the faith that justifies man before God has its outer
manifestation and proof in the works that herald it. Faith
divorced from deeds is lifeless as a corpse.

The life of prayer issues forth in a way of action dedicated to God. When his Spirit infuses our soul, we turn to him and become as he is. The uncreated light of God pours into the personality; as we confront it and are purified by it, so we are transformed from glory to glory by the Lord who is Spirit (2 Cor. 3.18). There is therefore no special time for prayer but rather a perpetual life of prayer. This means that when we are closest to our own authentic nature we are closest to God, and the divine name is on the lips of the soul. This name resounds in majesty through the soul and its echo reverberates in the marrow of the body as well as in the corridors of the mind. In this way the whole personality resonates to the glory of God, and the aspirations of the soul cry out in the prayer of Christ that we may all be one as he and the Father are one. Prayer transforms the human soul into something of the stature of Christ by freeing it from personal striving and leading it to the foothills of sincere, silent communion with God. When our petitions and confessions have come to their close, the silent contemplation of the soul continues and we stand naked before the glory of God. In such ecstasy our nakedness is as appropriate as would be the most glorious apparel, should we adorn ourselves with it for God's greater glory.

Since prayer cannot be limited to any scheme devised by the human will, but is the spontaneous outflowing of the soul in unending thanksgiving to God's loving presence within it, there is no certain or dogmatic scheme of praying. Nevertheless it is necessary, especially in the early part of a person's spiritual life, to set aside certain periods each day when the soul can commune without distraction with God. When we know him as an unfailing presence deep within us as well as the source of all creation immeasurably above us, we shall always be with him in clear consciousness and our work will be his work also. The object of special times of silence is to celebrate and strengthen the bond that links the conscious mind with God. In my experience the most effective time of willed silent communion with God is in the early morning shortly after arising from one's sleep. It is then that the mind is most alert, refreshed and free from disturbing emotions and anxious thoughts. Furthermore, if the mind is opened to the blessing of God in the silence of peace and acceptance early in the day, it will retain something of that blessing as it descends to the atmosphere of the market-place and is sullied by the psychic emanations of the many distraught, unhappy people whom one meets in a day's work. Prayer should be practised during periods set aside later in the day and in the evening also.

No one can instruct another person how exactly he ought to pray. At the most one can establish a few guide-lines so as to lead the aspirant to silence and peace within. Then one should retreat unobtrusively from the holy ground of the soul, and leave the aspirant in the far more expert care of the Holy Spirit. It is for this reason that one should always be wary of recommended techniques of praying. They can all too easily become an end in themselves so that the person begins quite unconsciously to worship prayer rather than God. The few real masters of the spiritual life whom it falls to one's good fortune to meet in the course of a lifetime are noted for their humility and their spiritual radiance. They appear to know even less than the aspirant, because they have put all conceit and pedantry behind them, and have become a pure transparent glass through which the light of God penetrates to the core of all whom they meet and counsel. Indeed, the true counsellor knows nothing except the presence of God within, who leads him as well as those who have come to him for help to a truth far greater than the summation of all human wisdom. To abandon all known paths of human expertise in the explosive silence of God is the way of wisdom. Its end is a new life in God in which the separative human nature is transfigured and brought to a full participation in the divine reality of unitive love.

As regards guide-lines for entering the inner silence of the soul, the most that can be said is that the whole personality should be filled with something that leads one to God. If that which edifies the soul is contemplated, the disturbing thoughts and disruptive emotions that play so dominant a part in everyday life will be gradually dispelled. The first step in attaining an inner emptiness from all personal desire is to fill the body and mind with all that is good and noble that comes from a source beyond itself. From a Christian point of view this source of goodness and nobility is the Bible. A slow reading, not so much in a spirit of discursive analysis as in meditative absorption, of a Psalm, or the Beatitudes of Christ, or one of the many healing miracles, to mention only a few of the treasures of this unsurpassed book, will bring the mind into alignment with the true self as one enters into the secret place and closes the door to worldly distraction. Variations on the theme of biblical meditation include the celebrated 'Jesus Prayer' of the Eastern Orthodox tradition, in which one repeats inwardly with the drawing in of the breath, after the words of the publican in Jesus' parable, 'Lord Jesus Christ, son of God, have mercy on me, a sinner' (Luke 18.13). Eventually this sentence centres on the single word 'Jesus' which is drawn into the heart in a spirit of deep devotion and reverence. In this way the holy name is admitted into the depth of one's soul and all other considerations are excluded from one's attention. Another variety of biblical meditation is the use of the rosary with which to meditate on the mysteries of the life and death of Christ. The method of using the Bible that is selected depends essentially on the temperament and tradition of the person; one way is no more correct or 'spiritual' than another. Those who are natural contemplatives can enter into the stillness of the secret place of the Most High simply and unfailingly by lifting their hearts, souls, minds and bodies heavenwards in rapt worship of the One who is beyond all names, concepts and attributes. This is mystical prayer, and the various ways of entering the silence through the use of the Bible or by the charismatic gift of tongues find their common end in the entry of the whole person into absolute quietness.

In this quietness the divine presence is revealed at the centre of the created universe. He is the centre and the periphery, the height and the depth, the totality and that which transcends all outer forms and physical limits. In his indwelling he transcends all forms; in his transcendence he lies closer to the heart of every creature than the creature does to himself. In this state of all-absorbing knowledge that is the peak of every intimate relationship in which the self is magnified in the love it shares with the other, God is all and in all. He is beyond form and substance—indeed no thing; and yet everything that exists owes its being to him that is beyond definition. 'By love may he be gotten and holden, but by thought never' as we read in *The Cloud of Unknowing*. It is to the unknown presence that is closer to us than our own identity, more easily available to those who wait in faith than any human relationship, that we offer ourselves in body and soul in contemplative prayer. It is to his service that we dedicate ourselves to be a living sacrifice for all the world. It is in losing ourselves as we know ourselves in worldly consciousness that we find ourselves as we are in the form of eternal beings. This is where prayer has its own validity, where the soul communes in the closest intimacy with God, where all human assertiveness and arrogance are not simply excluded but are also ultimately re-admitted in order to be re-created, transfigured and glorified. No wonder the wise spiritual director does not instruct anyone how to pray but simply remains silent in abject humility as that person enters into living fellowship with God and is transformed into a full human being in that transaction. 'Take off your shoes, for the place on which you stand is holy ground' (Exod. 3.5). That place is every place where the presence of God is known; it is here and now whenever we are fully aware. We read in Genesis 28.10−22 how God came to Jacob in a dream at a certain place between Beersheba and Haran: angels of God were ascending and descending a ladder extending from the ground up to heaven. God also was there standing over Jacob, the God of Abraham and Isaac his father. When Jacob awoke, he was amazed that God was in that place and he never knew it. But God is in every place; it is our feeble, barely used powers of perception that exclude his presence from our gaze. All ground is holy to those whose gaze is directed inwardly to the centre of the soul and heavenward to the eternal presence of the Most High, who both transcends and comprehends all physical dimensions. The movement inward to the soul is also heavenward.

When we know God we can never be lonely again, because his presence is unconditional and eternal. With him alone we can converse freely, and he sustains us even when we traverse the valley of the shadow of death. When God is at the centre of our lives, everything we do is invested with a meaning that far outshines any immediate significance of the moment. Prayer is the great adventure of the soul into the limitless reality of the divine. It starts in the silence of contemplation, and as the love of God pours into the soul, so our whole being

responds in a prayer of praise and thanksgiving. Then we
come to see how far we are from God because of our own
sinful nature. Like Isaiah in the Temple who saw the Lord
seated on a high throne with his train filling the sanctuary,
when we confront God we are aware of our own separation
from him through the selfishness of our private vision of life.
This awareness of sin is in essence an acknowledgement of
how continually we fall from the mark of excellence that God
has implanted in the depths of the soul. We nurture an
attitude that exalts the satisfaction of the ego above all things,
so that the more profound intimations of excellence that
inform the soul are repeatedly bypassed and ignored. We use
other people as things rather than revere them as human
beings created in God's image, and our communications with
them are all too often predatory, being concerned with what
we can get from them rather than how best we may serve
them. But just as Isaiah was cleansed from on high by the
angelic host that surrounded the Lord, so we too are cleansed
as we ascend the mountain of contemplation which is a
replica of the mountain where Jesus was transfigured and
spoke to the spirits of Moses and Elijah. As we confess our
sins and make petitions for the strength to master the
inadequacy that lies at the root of our selfish attitude to life,
so we are forgiven and strengthened for what lies ahead of us.
The prayer from the depth of a chastened heart proceeds in
contemplative silence, and is a real communication of the
soul with God. It is a deeply felt offering of the self to God in
unconditional service, the end of which is a renewed, healed
person that has emerged triumphantly from the pit of
suffering.

But the summation of that renewal and healing is no longer
purely personal; it now assumes a communal importance.
Therefore the prayers of confession and petition find their
conclusion in the prayer of intercession for all the world.

NINE

Remembering Others in Prayer

Prayer is the way in which the soul is infused by the power of the Holy Spirit. If one continues to pray in confidence and strength despite all outer diversions and inner discouragements, there will be a gradual change in one's disposition. The effect is neither rapid nor magical—growth, whether physical or spiritual, takes time and is unobtrusive when viewed on a day-to-day basis—but as one's life proceeds so one becomes dimly aware of an inner composure and tolerance to events that would previously have disturbed one's equilibrium. One reacts less abruptly to the insensitive intrusion of other people into one's thoughts and private life; one becomes less jealous when one hears of another's success in one's own chosen field; one responds with greater calm in the face of unpleasant circumstances that before would have shattered one emotionally to the extent of preventing one from working properly or being decently aware of other people in the neighbourhood. St Paul says to his disciples in Philippi: 'I wish you all joy in the Lord. I will say it again: all joy be yours. Let your magnanimity be manifest to all' (Phil. 4.4—5). This magnanimity is the fruit of intensive prayer. When the Spirit of the Lord is upon one, one thinks less about oneself and one's own safety and more about other people. This concern for others follows a healthy attitude to oneself. In this respect there is a profound difference between being self-centred and centred in the self. The self-centred person is aware of himself almost to the exclusion of other people. Everything he does has the final aim of exalting himself at the expense of others whom he uses quite unashamedly for his selfish purposes. And yet that person does not know himself, for if he did he would not need to strive so obsessively to establish and protect his own image in the world, an image that he erroneously identifies with his true being. The more he attains the more insecure he becomes, because he is entrapped in defending and maintaining that which is by its very nature ephemeral. By contrast, a person who is centred in the self projects his true identity wherever he finds himself and in whatever activity he is engaged. He knows himself for what he is—both a mere speck in the horizon of infinity and a living soul with God at its centre. In other words, he has no illusions about his insignificance as a personality but is constantly aware of the uniqueness of his contribution to the world as a servant of God. Being centred in his own being, he can radiate that unique presence to everyone and everything around him in an attitude of benediction. This is the way of blessing that we have previously touched upon.

One can know that inner self with the intimacy that comes of long familiarity best by the practice of long, devoted prayer. As one enters the secret place of the Most High, so one ceases to identify oneself with anything other than the Spirit of God set deeply in the soul. And this Spirit is universal. No living creature is without God's Spirit—indeed, that Spirit pervades the whole created universe so that nothing is outside its range or beneath its sustaining power and love. When we are in the Spirit that is of God we are truly in communion with all that lives, a communion that is not simply theoretical and theologically correct, but one also that binds us to everything that lives and suffers in ties of the strongest concern. This concern shows itself in self-giving love. St Paul says: 'Then throw off falsehood; speak the truth to each other, for all of us are the parts of one body' (Eph. 4.25). This 'membership one of another' is established at the level of soul or true self, for on the plane of the physical body we are clearly separate and divided. As we enter into the full domain of personality, so we leave behind the primitive, separative view of ourselves—a view that sees the person purely in terms of outer attributes so that one is judged as being superior or inferior to someone else. Instead we see ourselves in a mature light as living human beings in fellowship with each other and united in the Spirit of God, by whom the whole created universe is sustained. By that Spirit we are brought together into one body when we enter into the life of Christ, an entrance (a full baptism in essence) made definitively when we give of ourselves to the world as sacrifices for truth and service. Then we are fully members of the divine community whose head is Christ, and we become potent bearers of the Holy Spirit, transmitting that Spirit to all for whom we pray in unfailing fidelity. 'For where two or three have met together in my name, I am there among them' (Matt. 18.20).

This faithful remembrance of our fellow men is the basis of intercession, the interposing of oneself between God and the world seen in the form of the other person. It is the most immediately compelling part of one's prayer life because it is at once rigorously demanding, loving and far-reaching in its effects. Even a feeble prayer life may be sustained during fallow periods by the thought of other people's needs, those less fortunate than we are ourselves. Even when one feels completely exhausted and is assailed by the most testing agnosticism about the efficacy of one's prayer, or about prayer in general, a remembrance of those close to one will spur on one's prayer life. It is a fact of life that when all rational argument and psychological considerations point to the futility of spiritual exercises and the non-existence of a supersensual reality, the experience of the living God suddenly breaks in on one and shatters the intellectually unassailable edifice of unbelief that has temporarily held one imprisoned. Before the blast of the Holy Spirit, who blows where he wills so that no one can forecast his impetus or decree where he shall go, the rational limitations that proud men have erected of what is possible in our little world disintegrate in the fire of reality. Disappointment of our immediate worldly prospects may be necessary before we can experience the life-giving force of God's presence that reveals to us a completely different view of reality. When the rational is extended through the non-rational and the sensual illuminated by the supersensual, the life of prayer is shown to be the most real manifestation of God's grace in our lives. All things are indeed possible to those who believe: this is not a comment on the credulity of the masses to the claims of a charlatan, but a prediction of the work of the Holy Spirit in the lives of all who are open to the love of God in the moment at hand. It is in this respect that only those who can accept the Kingdom of God as a little child can enter it. When we have put away from ourselves all barriers of thought, whether of belief or non-belief, of naive credulity or hard scepticism, of desire for substantiation or pride in our own independence, and have entered the eternal present with chaste heart and innocent mind, the glory of God comes to meet us and we partake of the divine nature in which we were fashioned and to which we are destined to arrive in the presence and form of Christ. It is in this spirit alone that we can appreciate the promise of Jesus that the door is always opened to those who knock, that the seeker always finds what he is looking for, that he who asks always receives (Matt. 7.7). Our own arrogance occludes the power of God from our lives; complete silence in trusting love opens the door of the soul into which the living God can at last enter and re-create the creature in the form of his living Son.

The person living alone may be aware of a special responsibility, almost a vocation, towards praying for other people. Such intercessory prayer may be a solitary act or else may take place among a group of those with like mind. In fact, praying for others has both a solitary and a communal component. One cannot add one's power of concern to a group until one is inwardly attuned to the divine presence. On the other hand, the prayers of a group of loving people extend God's purpose in the world much more effectively than does the intercession of a single person, no matter how dedicated he may be. God's purpose is that we should all come to wholeness, to be healed and integrated as people. This is an essential preliminary event in the healing and integration of society. In this respect the spiritual life stresses the balance that must be struck between the growth into sanctity of the individual and the healing of the community. Those who live alone will have their efforts directed primarily to their own spiritual development, whereas the person who lives in a community will be concerned more about healthy relationships among people. There is a tendency nowadays to exalt the communal side of the Kingdom of God above the inner spiritual unfolding of the person, which is sometimes derisively dismissed as cultivating one's own soul in the luxury of a private domain while the world and its problems are insidiously dismissed from one's attention. In fact, the spiritual development of the individual is an essential precondition for the healing of society, but personal sanctity can never develop effectively or authentically except in the context of social concern. As I grow in spiritual strength, so I take with me all those around me with whom I communicate in a day's work. They are filled with the Spirit of God that radiates increasingly from me, while I, in giving myself unstintingly to my neighbour, am filled ever more generously with that Spirit. In the spiritual life the more one gives in the name of God, the more one receives from him. As St Paul puts it: 'The life I live is no longer my life but the life that Christ lives in me' (Gal. 2.19). The one who lives alone has, if he makes the most of his time, an especially great opportunity for growing into spiritual awareness. The corresponding responsibility for him is to make this gift of awareness available to his fellows by the practice of prayer and service. Indeed, when a person on his own sees the opportunities for spiritual growth that his way of life offers, he praises God for the privilege of being allowed to enjoy the divine favour and presence. Those who have no time for prayer have no time for life — and all too often it is those who are encumbered with the pressing needs of others on all sides that bow down before the apparent inevitability of a life devoid of silence with God. They may have to suffer a severe loss or bereavement before they can find time to speak to God in prayer. When all outer appurtenances are shriven from one, then alone may one have the undisturbed opportunity for communing with the source of all life who is also the sustainer of the life within one.

The two essential requirements for effective intercessions are a love of God and a love of one's fellow men. To intercede means in effect to be the instrument of God by which his Spirit may be conveyed to those in need. It is, I have no doubt, God's will that all people should be made whole, that indeed the intermediary law of decay and death that ends all mortal life should yield to the transfiguration of all matter into eternal spiritual substance. The presage of this final, cataclysmic transformation was shown in the resurrection of the physical body of Jesus to full spiritual radiance — glimpsed during his transfiguration and finally witnessed at the time of his resurrection. But for this healing to occur the will has to be made active. It has to affirm its own compliance in the work of transfiguration. In our world, God acts through his creatures, namely human beings. These are blessed with the gifts of intellectual understanding and spiritual vision that have been, as far as we can tell, withheld from the remainder of the animal creatures of our planet. The will of the human being is free to act according to the inner judgement of the true self. Unfortunately only a few people can function at that deep level of authenticity for any considerable length of time. When we act at the level of ego consciousness, the will is deflected by every outside stimulus and inner impulse. It is no wonder that many psychologists deride the concept of a free, independent will, and in respect of most people this scepticism is soundly based. But when the elements of the personality have been controlled by a more authoritative centre of consciousness, which is the true self, or soul, the will is no longer as subject to the fluctuations of inner emotional conflict or the vicissitudes of external events as it was previously. At last it can assume some mastery over the personality and act with responsibility and freedom. This fulfilled acting of the will is achieved during contemplation, when the inner gaze of the person is directed to the transcendent God who also, paradoxically, is at home in the soul's centre.

It is at this stage that the human will can, at least to some extent, know the divine will and work together with it rather than in opposition to it—a train of events that reverses the usual antagonism of good and evil tendencies in the personality that St Paul so bitterly lamented in Romans 7.14–25, as we have already noted, and finds its original description in the myth of the Fall described in Genesis 3. When the will can bring the mind to inner stillness in the act of contemplation, it can make the person ready to listen to God and play his part in the process of universal healing. It therefore follows that the act of intercessory prayer is one in which we remember the person in need with tenderest solicitude in the depths of silent communion, so that the Spirit of God can touch the soul of that person and effect such healing as is appropriate. The degree of healing attained depends on the will of the person to receive love—not everyone wants to be healed—and the degree of sickness. In the most impressive examples of healing that follow prayer, the improvement is slow, progressive and complete. Dramatic answers to intercessory prayer, though very acceptable when they take place, are not always long-lasting. A slow, integrated healing of the whole personality is ultimately preferable to a sudden dramatic cure that may leave the person spiritually and mentally unprepared. The end-result of such imperfect healing is often a relapse into ill-health once again, possibly of a type different from the original complaint.

In the periods of prayer that should mark our special communion with God, it is wise to intercede for others after we have prayed for ourselves in confession and petition. It may seem somewhat selfish to think about our own needs first, but in fact until we have started to get ourselves in order, our concern for other people is likely to be of little avail. Jesus instructs us, in his lightness born of innate godliness, to remove the plank from our own eyes first before we meddle officiously to remove specks from the eyes of other people. As he reminds us, only when our own vision is clear can we see properly to help other people (Matt. 7.3—5). This advice, obvious enough on a physical level, is even more true spiritually. If we are to pray effectively for other people, we have to get ourselves out of the way, so that the Holy Spirit is not deflected by our wishes and prejudices, nor coloured by our own inadequacies. Of course, if this injunction were to be taken literally, none of us would ever be fit to pray for others! But fortunately even making an attempt at one's own inner cleansing through confession and petition allows us to be a fit instrument on whom God's grace can work and from whom his Spirit may flow to those in need.

In praying for others it is most important to be centred on the love of God in one's heart and the person in need in one's inner eye. Love should flow from the intercessor to the person prayed over. It is of no consequence that this person is often unknown to us, a mere name in fact. God knows him—and this is enough. Indeed, it is often more efficacious to pray for someone who is a stranger than for a close friend or relative. The reason is that in interceding for an unknown person we can remain non-attached, and allow the work of the Holy Spirit to proceed unhindered by our emotional interference. On the other hand, when we pray for someone close to us, our own passionate desire for his recovery according to our own understanding and demands tends to interpose itself between God's will and what he knows is best for our loved one. If we are unwise enough to try to 'broadcast' improving thoughts telepathically to the one for whom we are praying, we may do positive harm, for then we will be usurping the place and function of God. Since few of us have much insight into our own character and its problems, it is hardly surprising that, when we decree what is best spiritually or psychologically for someone else, the results are likely to be disastrous. The correct attitude for intercession is a trusting calm with which to co-operate with God, to which is added a deep concern for all who are in need of prayer. In that state of watchful calm one seems to know the other person merely by articulating his or her name in the deepest recesses of the mind. In the words of Psalm 42.7: 'Deep calls to deep in the roar of thy cataracts, and all thy waves, all thy breakers, pass over me.' One does not need to visualize that person so much as to commune with his soul in the depths of one's own soul, an inner action impossible to describe rationally any more than the experience of God or of falling in love can be discursively analysed. It is known because it changes one's life and adds a new meaning to existence.

When one is deep in prayer, especially the prayer of intercession, it is not unusual for a light, sometimes a warm glow, to appear before one's closed eyes (it is usual to close one's eyes in prayer so as to avoid visual distractions from outside). This light may be pure white or it may have a more definite colour; in my experience it often has a deep blue tint. I mention this simply to allay disquiet in the newcomer to prayer who may encounter this psychico-spiritual pheno- menon and be alarmed or entranced by it. It is not to be confused with the uncreated light of God's emergent energies that rarely presents itself to the saint in prayer. At any rate it is at the very least harmless and at most an added grace to the life of prayer. This light may help us in directing our love to those for whom we pray. But it must not be sought after, for then it could become the end of prayer instead of a grace of the internal life. In the deepest contemplation there is no such light, only bliss. Above all, one should not purposely invoke light in prayer for this, like telepathic interference with the one prayed over, enters the realm of magic. God is subtly excluded and the psychic power of the ego is substituted. In this respect magic is the use of occult, psychic forces for selfish purposes. Its end is invariably deleterious, no matter how well motivated the practitioner believes himself to be. The heart, as Jeremiah reminds us, is the most deceitful of all things, and desperately sick (Jer. 17.9). Only when the heart, the emotional pivot of the personality, is chastened and cleansed by the power of the Holy Spirit does it cease to do evil and start to do good.

When one is rapt in prayer the soul, that deep seat of consciousness, is lifted up to God in Christ by the power of the Holy Spirit. The essential action of the will is to keep the person in a state of watchful, alert silence. In other words, one *does* nothing in order to *be* everything. One is not 'taken over' by the Spirit of God as in a state of trance. One is inspired and transfigured by that Spirit so as to become a real person, something eventually of the measure of Christ's stature. Then one can work in confident collaboration with God through the power of his Spirit, in company, I have no doubt, with the full Communion of Saints and the Ministry of Angels. These intermediary powers are fearlessly affirmed in the Christian creeds and liturgies (the angelic host is acknowledged magnificently in the context of the Eucharist together with all the company of heaven), but their objective existence seems to be real to the few rather than the many. When we are in rapt contemplation, giving of ourselves unstintingly to God's service, our spiritual eyes may be opened, as they were to Elisha's servant (2 Kings 6.7), and the vast spiritual concourse of heaven, where all dwell in peace and union with God, may be shown to us. Needless to say, such a revelation is not to be looked for; the will of God and the service of our fellow creatures are what should be perpetually in our minds. These are the objects of our searchings, not the intermediary psychico-spiritual realms. But what may be shown to us in the course of our spiritual work is an added grace which has the benefit of lightening the burden of mundane unbelief that we, as citizens of the world, have inevitably to bear.

As our personalities are opened to the divine energies that flow from the Holy Spirit, so our souls are united in the love of God with those whom we call to mind by name. The Holy Spirit will then lighten the darkness of all for whom we pray. It is not necessary for those who are the object of our intercession to know that they are being prayed for, but nevertheless this awareness of prayer can be of enormous support to a believer who is very ill, or has recently undergone a major surgical operation, or is emotionally distraught because of some personal tragedy. What is needed is that the person who is prayed for should not be obstructive to the love of God. That conscious co-operation is not essential for efficacious prayer is testified to in the remarkable effects that may be seen in young children (and also loved animals) who are ill and subsequently recover. In these instances, though the one prayed for could not even begin to understand what was being done to him by the power of God working through devoted human instruments, there would be no emotional or intellectual barrier to that power as it pervaded the deepest recesses of the mind. On the other hand, people who are full of resentment and bitterness of soul—and some such may be found among conventional church-goers who feel that they deserve preferential treatment from the Almighty because of their loyalty to his cause—may positively inhibit the healing power of God entering them. Until such a person has relented of his rebellious attitude and is prepared to enter the future devoid of all preconceptions and demands for justice—in fact like the little child who alone can receive the Kingdom of Heaven—the healing power of love will not be able to penetrate his soul, which lies deeply hidden behind dense clouds of antagonism, indignation and anger. It is important to realize that while it is contingent on us to love everyone, we cannot force anyone to accept our love. Only patience and self-effacing persistence will make our message of recon-ciliation eventually acceptable to one whose heart is hard and unyielding. This stoniness of heart, about which Ezekiel speaks so forcibly, is sometimes due to suffering and injustice borne by the person in his earliest childhood, with the result that he is now incapable of receiving anything with trust; he believes that everyone who shows an interest in him wants to take advantage of him and betray him.

The obdurate hostility that confronts us in some people, though a serious barrier to effective intercessory prayer, should not, however, deter us from praying assiduously for them. No one is eternally beyond the power of God's redeeming love, but only a long ministry of patience and forbearance can prevail in the presence of strong negative emotions. God himself stands patiently at the door of many souls and knocks for admittance. If he has had to wait for many years to be welcomed into the personality, we should not be too disappointed at our own initial poor showing! But we must persist in faith.

In remembering others in prayer the mind is focused in calm acceptance on the name of the person in trouble. It is unnecessary, indeed unproductive, to muster up feelings of concern and love. The love that is real comes from God, not ourselves, and irradiates our souls with such warmth that it flows from us to others when we confront them simply and without affectation. The act of focusing need not take long; it is the intensity of prayer that matters far more than the length of time taken. A contemplative can be in communion with the whole world within a few seconds, whereas one unschooled in the inner life can spend hours shifting around in body and mind, and still be as far from his centre, the secret place within, as he was when he started. When there are a fair number of people to be prayed for, it is particularly important not to expend too much time on any one of them, but rather to apportion a period of, say, ten to fifteen seconds to each. Of course, no one in prayer would measure time in this way, but the indication from the Spirit of God would be towards intensity and brevity rather than diffuseness and length of time. Jesus reminds us in another context not to go on babbling to God like the heathen, who imagine that the more they say, the more likely they are to be heard. In fact our Father knows what our needs are before we ask him (Matt. 6.7−8). In the same way, when we are in rapt prayer, God's Spirit goes to those in need as soon as we remember them; it is not necessary to persist for minutes on end in the communication. On the other hand, the use of long lists of names placed impersonally on a table is not to be recommended, since the human contact is severely diluted in the process. The name should be enunciated as that of the unique person whom it represents; it should be regarded in love and reverence. It is indeed a privilege to intercede for another person.

Some people will require intercessory prayer for many months, others for only a few days. When one appears to forget a name it usually means that the Holy Spirit is telling one that special prayer is no longer necessary. Indeed, it is contingent on those who ask for our prayers to keep us informed about their progress or that of their loved one in danger. If they lack the interest and courtesy to perform this small act of acknowledgement, they prove themselves unworthy of the prayers that they have requested. The reward in store for those that give of their services to others in prayer and other spiritual labour is not financial; it is the joy of seeing 'a brother who was dead and has come back to life, who was lost and is found' (Luke 15.32). This work will continue as long as we are alive, and it becomes a central activity for all who live alone. By it more than in any other way, one ceases to be alone any longer, but instead becomes the centre of an ever-enlarging circle of associates, friends and brothers.

Furthermore, one should remember people who are in need as often as possible, not only during periods of silence given over specially to communion with God but also when one is alone in the day's activity. Whenever one remembers a person in concern and loving tenderness one is praying for him. To give of oneself in intense solicitude to one's brother is an authentic act of prayer. But such unobtrusive prayer at street-corners (in contrast to the ostentatious prayers so derided by Jesus as an act of hypocrisy in Matthew 6.5) comes best from the lips of the mind and soul of the one who is schooled in the interior spiritual life. When we remember our friends in need in the depths of prayer, we will continue to bear them in mind even when we are about the day's tumultuous business.

Intercessory prayer should also embrace the larger concerns of the world, especially world peace. But first let us remember individual people before we move on to the greater world. It is far easier to pray for people whom we know than for vast organizations that cannot but remain anonymous blocks of humanity to us until we have entered deeply into the spirit of intercession. When we are at peace in ourselves following the prayers of confession and petition, and are one with our neighbours in intercession, only then will our hearts be so open and our souls so vibrant with love that we will be able to embrace whole peoples, organizations and nations in our solicitude before God. We should also remember that our prayers, always vitally important, for peace among the world's nations will ring more true and have greater effect when we are at peace in ourselves and with our families, colleagues and neighbours than when we are at loggerheads with our little world and in turmoil within ourselves. It is once more a matter of clearing our own sight before we endeavour to show other people the way. It is, I believe, for this reason that so much intercessory prayer formulated with moving eloquence during religious services of various kinds seems to make so little impression on the world's precarious situation. We seem to hope, in a regression to childish ways of thought, that God will somehow be induced to act on our behalf if we speak fulsomely enough to him in prayer. In fact, he acts through us, his agents, in this world of matter. Only as we are healed, can we participate in the healing of the nations of which we ourselves are members. Our help indeed comes only from the Lord, Maker of heaven and earth (Psalm 121.2), but we have to play our part in bringing that help down to the realm of practical life and international peace.

Intercession plays, I believe, a greater part in bringing about world peace than we shall ever grasp. Only when the minds of the people, and especially their rulers in whom is invested terrifyingly great power of life and death, are filled with thoughts of love and reconciliation instead of fear and revenge, will the nations turn from preparations for war to the activities of peace. Only when the heart is moved from the isolation of self-preservation to the openness of self-giving on behalf of others will the person progress from warlike activities of extermination to the life-giving practice of creative art and social reconstruction. Those of us who pray day by day, tirelessly devoted to the service of God and our fellow men, are acting on the deepest level to change the fundamental attitude of those who govern states and nations. On the work of intercession may depend the future survival of our world. The little ones who live alone act with the great contemplative communities in this work of transfiguration.

TEN

The Way of Service

The fulfilment of living is service. When we seek for ourselves, the end is disillusionment and death. When we seek the happiness and welfare of others, we grow into an organism immeasurably greater than our own insignificant selves. Indeed, we attain to something of the measure of a perfect man, seen as the likeness of Christ. As St Paul reminds us: 'We brought nothing into the world; for that matter we cannot take anything with us when we leave, but if we have food and covering we may rest content' (1 Tim. 6.7—8). The acquisition of worldly things, though not in itself reprehensible, becomes demonic when objects dominate our attention to the extent that riches and possessions become symbols of security. I say that acquiring wealth and power is not in itself evil because the things of this world are our means of growth and self-realization. The Parable of the Talents (Matt. 25.14—30) can no doubt be interpreted on various levels, but it continues to have an important mundane application: we must use and husband the world's resources for our own and others' gain. This gain is more than merely making a financial profit; it is a development of the powers of body, mind and soul that are usually alternatively squandered in reckless living and allowed to lie dormant while we lapse into dank apathy and let the world go heedlessly by. By participating in the world's affairs we gain something far greater than money and power: we attain an adult maturity based on a capacity to manage our earthly affairs responsibly and with concern for others.

Nor do the things of this world lose by intelligent human stewardship on their behalf. They are raised up from being mere material objects with only a finite life span in front of them to something of the nature of eternal values that will persist in the spiritual world long after their physical form has disintegrated. Anything consecrated to God and our fellow men undergoes a subtle inner change that is a distant presage of the resurrection of all matter into the spiritual body of Christ. This will be enacted on the 'last day' when Christ comes again to us in a form that all of us will instantly recognize as being of God. At present it is enacted whenever a priest consecrates the bread and wine of the Eucharist so that they, while remaining themselves, are also changed into the body and blood of Christ. The whole question of the relationship of what we call the material with the spiritual is still a mystery to minds incarcerated in a purely physical understanding of reality. But there is enough evocative evidence to suggest that mind has a direct effect on matter in addition to the indirect influence it exerts through rational activity. An unpleasant example of the direct effect of mind over matter is the poltergeist activity that proceeds psychically from emotionally disturbed adolescents in exceptional circumstances. A more acceptable manifestation is the phenomenon of psychic healing, but far better is the truly spiritual healing that proceeds from the mind of God by the power of the Holy Spirit through his ministers to those who require help. Intercessory prayer is another example of healing, this time performed at a distance, that comes from God to the one prayed for. As we grow in spiritual grace, so the work of the Holy Spirit will become a natural part of our ministry, and this will show itself not only in more harmonious human relationships but also, I believe, in a more evenly balanced cosmic atmosphere. By this I mean a world less subject to natural disasters such as floods and droughts, hurricanes and earthquakes. To some people this view of the power of human emotions on the physical conditions of our planet will seem simplistic, but those who are aware of the power of psychic phenomena may be less tempted to dismiss the thought out of hand. All this, at any rate, stresses the sacred quality of all relationship, not only human but also material. How we treat our possessions is of an importance that outweighs their material value, for they too are a part of the divine providence.

But the most immediately important service is that which we give to other people. When our human relationships are in order we shall begin to respond in brotherly love to all that lives and to conserve our natural environment as a sacred duty not only for our survival but also for its transformation. How best can we serve our neighbour? By giving of ourselves to him in respectful attention. Service involves three motions: attention, deliberation and action. It does not mean simply doing something at all costs. Sometimes the greatest service we can render is merely to support a person with our attention and concern so that he can muster his own resources and do the appropriate work or make the right decision. Officious interference with the lives of other people in the guise of serving them is a common way of eluding the responsibilities in our own life, or deflecting our attention from our own inner deficiencies on to the troubles of another person. But if we can give of our most valuable commodity to someone, we can initiate the transformation in that person of diffidence to faith, of apathy to vibrant interest and concern. Our most valuable gift is our attention. It is much more important to give a person who is in need our own presence than a large amount of money or possessions. It could be argued that a starving man would prefer food to my presence and concern, but until I can confront that person and give him my full attention, I shall remain ignorant of his deepest needs. The relief of an immediately pressing problem, though of burning urgency, is best brought about by the one who has a wider vision of the person's requirements than by those who see him merely as a body to be fed. Man indeed cannot live on bread alone, but on every word that God utters (Matt. 4.4). The word of God is contained in Holy Scripture, and its central focus is eternal love. I can give a person alms while despising him in my heart and taking care to contaminate myself as little as possible with his presence. But when I give a person my attention, the barrier between us is narrowed so that eventually I shall be able to understand even the most difficult individual. Those who are emotionally disturbed, mentally unbalanced or obsessed with a particular enthusiasm that takes control of their entire life are especially difficult to tolerate when we are in low, earthly consciousness. They are simply a nuisance from whom we would wish to detach ourselves forthwith. But if we can listen to them in patience and forbearance, something of our spirit, that is constantly filled with the Holy Spirit, may penetrate their consciousness. As a result, they may be able to effect a more creative relationship with other people than they had ever previously enjoyed.

The person living alone has, if his life is to be fulfilled, to be much more open to other people than he was previously. This is the first step in filling the void of companionless existence that lies ahead of most of us but especially the solitary person who can look forward to little practical help from those around him in his present desolation. To be open to another person is the first step in knowing him and eventually serving him. It is a way of relationship especially available to the person who lives alone. Many such people on their own would confess complete ineptitude in dealing with others in distress; their own way of life is hardly sociable, at least on a worldly, superficial level, and they would seem the least qualified to relieve the fear and loneliness of their compatriots. But when we feel most inadequate in being able to help someone else, provided we acknowledge this helplessness silently to God and call upon his omnipresent Spirit, our own minds will be filled with wisdom apposite to the situation in which we now find ourselves. And from our secret lips the knowledge of eternal things may issue forth. The less we feel we are, the more useful we may find ourselves in God's service. After all, only the one who knows his lack and has been shriven of all illusions of importance by the cold truth of failure and loneliness is able to enter with authority into the lives of other unhappy people. And the more we know of real life—as opposed to the glamorous surface that passes for success—the more we realize how close we all are in bonds of fear, disillusionment and spiritual dereliction. Indeed, to be made aware of this inner void is the beginning of the spiritual life. As the Wisdom writers of the Old Testament so often tell us: 'The fear of the Lord is wisdom, and to turn from evil is understanding' (Job 28.28).

This availability to listen and hear what other people are saying is the authentic way of getting to know them. Eventually we hear with our whole being and effect a deeper psychic communion with them, soul speaking to soul. The end of the work is a spiritual fellowship in God. It comes about therefore that the way of service is the most certain way of effecting a deep relationship with other people, and I repeat once more that the heart of service is availability to give attention, listen, hear and then communicate in word, action and prayer. The way of service has two components. The first is the inner path of intercessory prayer. Its reverse, worldly side is giving of oneself in the actions of availability. To help another person is a very great privilege. But before we can undertake such a bold step we have to get the ego out of its customary seat of dominance so that a more profound spiritual centre of awareness can direct the personality according to the will of God. When I try to do good, I end by dictating to the one I hope to help. When I strive to be still and know the all-pervading love of God, a strength of purpose flows from the depths of my being that amazes me by its excellence and charity. This previously unknown depth of service can show itself in the most unpromising individual when his compassion is evoked in an emergency. While St Paul's spiritual diagnosis of the poor moral condition of the natural man cannot be surpassed — that he does the evil that he eschews with his mind, while failing to do the good that he so admires (Rom. 7.14 − 25) − it is nevertheless true also that there is a spark of divinity in all of us, Christ in us, the hope of a glory to come (Col. 1.27). When we are called on in an emergency, this spark radiates through the grey mist of self-interest and sloth that usually obscures the true self, or soul, of the individual, so that the whole person shines with something of the supernatural light of God. He may perform actions of unwonted nobility and self-sacrifice, even to the extent of being prepared to sacrifice his life for a stranger in peril. Once we move beyond the comfortable limits set by the worldly-wise for our prosperity and self-preservation, we enter into a world of spirituality in which sacrifice is the way to self-actualization and death the portal to eternal life. The person on his own, if he is open to the power of the Holy Spirit in contemplative prayer, will soon know of the presence of the risen Christ in his life. When we confront death in calm acceptance and allow the warm pulse of life to drive us on to the mastery of the self and the service of others, a new way of life is revealed to us. The things of this world are seen to be mere shadows on the way to self-mastery, while the eternal challenge of spiritual values becomes the driving impulse of our existence.

To be of service to others on a practical level, the first

action is, as I have already stated, to be still and listen to them. This in itself is no mean achievement in the world of haste and bustle that we inhabit. The specialized agencies that exist to care for people in need—medical, psycho-therapeutic, sociological—tend to put their patients or clients in special categories who can then be dealt with in ways that are appropriate to their condition. To label and categorize a person is, no doubt, necessary for his proper treatment as a clinical case or a psychological or social problem, but in the end his essential uniqueness as an individual is severely diluted by this process. The specialized agencies of healing can dehumanize those with whom they operate if they forget or neglect the uniqueness of their clients. This is where a spiritual approach to personality is vitally important: that man was made in the divine image and his end is to partake fully of the divine nature. Alleviating a medical, psychological or social problem is a very necessary step in bringing a person to his full potential, but if it does not affirm him as a human being in his own right, the step leads to a decline into uselessness, disillusionment and final disintegration. 'Where there is no vision, the people perish' (Prov. 29.18).

A person on his own can complement the work done by specialists in bringing relief to suffering humanity simply by being available to speak to them on a personal level and take an interest in their apparently trivial hopes and fears, trivial at any rate to the high-powered worker whose mind is often filled with his own research projects to the exclusion of lesser things. One may be so obsessed with grandiose schemes for healing humanity that one loses sight of its individual members. The art of healing is simple in essence though profound in its implication. It consists in the ability, to quote Isaiah 61.1 — 2, of bringing good news to the humble, binding up the broken-hearted, proclaiming liberty to captives and releasing those in prison. The year of the Lord's favour is proclaimed, and (in the addition quoted in Luke 4.18) sight is recovered for the blind. This work is the province of the Holy Spirit and not primarily of human ingenuity and expertise. It is brought about by the agent of healing sitting peacefully with the person who needs help and speaking to him in a quiet, considered dialogue. The one in need opens himself in full confidence, a confidence born of friendship, to the one

with whom he communicates. The person who helps has no
ready-made solutions to his problems; indeed, real human
problems are seldom, if ever, solved by the intellect alone, but
by the power of God guiding one on through the darkness of
daily living until a light suddenly appears in the distance and
understanding breaks into the previously uncomprehending
mind. It is similar in its own way to a journey undertaken
through the impenetrable darkness of a moonless night until
the distantly appearing first rays of the sun herald the start of
a new day. We continue bravely in the dark night because we
know that the dawn is ever more closely within our vision.
Likewise we struggle on in the darkness because we are
imbued with a spiritual light of belief that assures us that all
will be well in the end for those who love God (Rom. 8.28).
The person who is with us in our darkness and supports us
with his faith adds his quota to our confidence and fills us
with hope. If such a friend has specialized knowledge of
psychology so much the better, but an absence of training
need not deter one from serving those who are in difficulties.
The warm, silent hospital visitor plays his part also in
accelerating the recovery of a patient after a major surgical
operation or a severe illness. It is not so much what one says
that matters—indeed the wise visitor learns to be silent, lest
he burdens the one in pain with his own problems—but what
one radiates in love and faith. Starting this elementary healing
ministry is in itself a pure act of faith, since none of us knows
what the future holds in store. But as we persist in the way,
so an inner assurance is vouchsafed us, and we begin to
divine the welcoming light that lies at the end of the dark
tunnel of the present distress.

Faith in the unknown future, whether of this life or the life
beyond death, comes as one treads the way. So-called proofs
that are sought by consulting those who claim prophetic or
psychic knowledge are seldom convincing and often very
confusing. But as we move with courage into the unknown,
so a light shows itself around our feet, guiding us on until the
hidden way is clearer to us than our own identity. And that
light eventually illuminates every particle of our body and
radiates from the depth of the soul until we do indeed glimpse
our full identity, that of a son of God made in the image of
Christ. What we show in ourselves we make manifest in

others also, and the end is a real healing of the person and finally of all society. This great universal healing takes place when all individuals play their part in spreading the light that comes from God, so that the world is illuminated and the whole creation is freed from the shackles of mortality to enter into the glorious liberty and splendour of the children of God, as St Paul describes in Romans 8.21. It is an awesome thought that this final transfiguration and resurrection of the world is brought about initially by simple, apparently unschooled, unimportant people giving of their essence in prayer and service to their fellow men. This service is paramount in the spiritual advancement of all people; no one is more advantageously placed than the person who lives alone, and can give of himself unsparingly to those who need someone to listen to them and reveal the love that comes to us from God when we are still and attentive.

Service, of course, does have a more executive aspect than this. In the passage from St James's letter that was quoted in a previous chapter, faith is seen to be substantiated by the works that proceed from it. If a brother is starving or naked, our first duty is to feed and clothe him. Merely listening to his tragedy is useless if our attention and compassion do not flow out in positive acts of charity. It follows therefore that we should be available to help a person in need with practical assistance as well as moral and spiritual support in prayer and conversation. The amount any individual can do is obviously dependent on his means; most of us can be of best help to those in need by supporting those larger agencies that exist to relieve poverty, disease and mental distress. This is where voluntary help in hospitals, prisons or institutions for the mentally disturbed is so important. But once again it is the personal touch that matters. The devoted helper is, after all, a very small unit in a vast organization, but the unit can articulate with other units in a way that, inevitably, impersonal organizations cannot. We tend to think that the problems of society are so enormous and their origins so intricate that simpletons like ourselves can contribute little of real help to their solution. But as soon as we get involved in the problems of even one family, we at once enter into the vast, impersonal world of suffering, and by our presence we imbue it with a spark of humanity. The common touch, the compassionate hand on the shoulder, the shared awareness of the glory and the tragedy of the present moment bring something of God into a situation of hopelessness, and a light begins to shine in the darkness of despair and touch it with a ray of hope. No one knows this better than the person who has had to live on his own for a long time, and has had shafts of spiritual light infused into the apparently meaningless journey of his life. And then he sees the light of purpose, and he goes on in joyous courage and determination to the work ahead of him.

The way of service that initiates a true healing ministry is, as has already been mentioned, laid down in the first verses of Isaiah 61. Good news is brought to the poor and humble, that they count as people, that God cares for them. The initial proof of God's care is the love that flows out to them from the minister of healing. We love because God loved us first, and the love of God is transmitted from ourselves, whom we must first love with all our defects and inadequacies, to those around us. It must be stressed that love cannot be manufactured; it is a free gift of God. If I try to love a person I will inevitably condescend to him, and my affection will have a palpably unreal quality. Soon the object of my 'love' will wince at my approach, while I will find that I really despise him. But if I open myself to the love of God, I will gradually change inwardly as a person, and I will begin to flow out in real concern to a considerable range of people. The reason for this is that I will approach them at soul level and my heart will be open to their hopes and fears, their glories and tragedies. And then I shall be their friend, just as they will be my friends: as I give of myself, so I receive the other. And the other is Christ, who shows himself perpetually in the stranger who walks along with me on my own particular Emmaus road. The final good news to be proclaimed to the little ones in God is that the Kingdom of Heaven is theirs, that their end is deification, the participation fully in the divine nature as seen in Christ.

The broken-hearted are bound up so that the disintegration they knew previously, when someone or something of priceless value was removed from their lives, is now healed through the self-giving of the servant in God. To support a person during the depth of his bereavement is a great privilege and a testimony to the sustaining power of love in restoring to wholeness the one whose previous purpose in living has been shattered. We have to go on alone after someone close to us has departed from us, but if we know that there is even one person who cares deeply about us and is available when the grief is intolerable, we can proceed in courage with our own lives. To be sure, this movement is painful and apparently purposeless, but as we progress, so a deeper meaning to life asserts itself: we too are to grow into the measure of the stature of a perfect man as seen in Christ (Eph. 4.13).

'How lovely on the mountains are the feet of the herald who comes to proclaim prosperity and bring good news, the news of deliverance, calling to Zion "Your God is King" ' (Isa. 52.7). This beautiful passage summarizes the work of the servant who brings the good news of deliverance from past woe and the prosperity that finds an inexhaustible supply of riches in God. For in God alone lies our rest and our strength.

Liberty is proclaimed to the captives, and those in prison are released. The real prison is our own mind, full of past conditioning that will not let the whole person be himself. The prison to which the vast majority of people in the world are confined is composed of the bricks and mortar of prejudice, ignorance, fear and a distorted view of the self. When we begin to learn that we are valued by God for ourselves alone irrespective of colour, race, social position or intellectual eminence, we can at last relax in his unfailing providence. It is the work of the servant, who is also the minister of healing, to expose the one he visits and counsels to the full thrust of acceptance and brotherhood in God. There is an important place for the physical embrace in this acceptance, since we relate to those around us with the body as well as the mind. Society tends to put its members into categories based on such external criteria as wealth, social distinction, education and occupation. In some societies a person's accent immediately identifies him with a particular social and educational class. When we are free from the subtle, insidious, evil prison of human discrimination, we begin to act as real human beings, as willed creatures of God. In fact, the ultimate key to liberty is such a severe tragedy in one's life that the suffering which accrues from it tears off the masks that previously hid one's true nature in a costume of make-believe. At last the soul is exposed, and its natural tendency is to turn to Christ, because it was created in the image of God. Only the one who has suffered knows the full extent of love and is capable of giving unreservedly of himself in love to his neighbour.

The blind see when the servant who visits them tears away the old prejudices and fears that had occluded their sight. When Jesus healed the man born blind, he opened not only his physical eyes but also the eyes of his soul. This is the inner eye that detects the reality that lies hidden behind the façade of surface activities. He was able to say 'All I know is this: once I was blind, now I can see' (John 9.25) and again 'If that man had not come from God he could have done nothing' (John 9.33). The religious authorities remained blind in spirit, because their prejudice against Jesus prevented them seeing spiritual truth. This blindness based on past patterns of belief prevents so many of us from understanding what our brothers are saying to us in the depth of their being. It also prevents us communicating with others in complete self-giving honesty. The service that the one on his own has to give the blind has two parts. He must aid the physically blind in his struggle for existence—and in this context the blind include that vast population who are incapacitated by various physical defects ranging from poor sight and hearing to lameness and paralysis—by helping to provide food and comfort for those in need. And he must also be the way in which the blind man sees a new purpose in his own life, that his negative feeling of resignation and despair may be transformed into a positive response of acceptance and hope. This hope is not so much for physical healing—which cannot be demanded—as that his life does, after all, have a really constructive basis and that the work he has done, and is doing, will play its part in the redemption of society. Those who can only stand and wait also have their glorious moment of service, like the three women who stood at the foot of the cross, supporting Jesus in unspoken love while the remainder of the spectators passed by in dull incomprehension. It has to be faced that, for every noble soul seeking to relieve the distress of the dark planet that is our little world, there are legions of the uncomprehending whose lives are controlled by destructive thoughts and lustful passions. But their time of redemption will come too, when they will learn that life is more than a garish procession of sensual entertainments. This knowledge will come to them when darkness occludes their physical and mental sight. And in the depths of their despair they too will see the suprasensual light of God in Christ. Then they too will begin to live as fully conscious human beings. Those who live alone are the precious light-bearers of God to the ones who live in the darkness of hell. 'The people who walked in darkness have seen a great light: light has dawned upon them, dwellers in a land as dark as death' (Isa. 9.2). The little ones in God are the precursors, the forerunners, of the new Advent when Christ will indeed be all and in all, as St Paul saw in Colossians 3.11. What is theologically true has yet to be made real in the life of the community where there are still unfortunately racial, social and educational differences that separate man from man. What is required is not a dull uniformity but a transcendence of the limitations of the individual person so that each one of us shows the power of Christ in his own life. Then will the ego be transfigured to the identity of the spirit within the soul, and one will be able to say with Christ, 'I and the Father are one'. It is to this far-off yet well heralded event that the whole creation moves.

It therefore follows that the service best rendered by those who live alone is being open to all classes of people. This openness invites them to share their hopes and aspirations as well as their fears and forebodings with us who are easy listeners. But *discretion* is an essential part of service, *the discretion that keeps the secrets of other people inviolate in our care*, and the discretion to know how far we may proceed with our help and when to call upon the more specialized agencies of assistance. The one who is a true minister of healing does not take the credit on himself; he knows how to share the honours with other helpers more skilled than he is in some special expertise. Service for others means bringing them into our family—in the case of the lone-dweller this is a family of one. But the family grows as those are added who play their part in spreading light and bestowing love on others. Prayer that is not made manifest in outer service to others becomes an unreal ritual that assumes the slavery of a superstitious drudgery. Service that is not fertilized by prayer becomes egocentric and tyrannical towards the ones we wish to assist. To get the ego out of its customary seat of domination into its fitting role of servant to the soul is the beginning of effective service to the world. The end of that service is the establishment of the divine community in the world. This community exists wherever we may find ourselves, and the apparently unpromising people around us are its hallowed members.

The key to effective service is self-forgetfulness. When we have set aside thoughts of our own unworthiness, ineptitude and lack of knowledge and start to do the healing act of caring sufficiently for a fellow sufferer in need, we have entered into the way of service. Experience teaches; indeed it is the only authentic teacher. The hints we may acquire on the way from specialist sources are often invaluable, but they can be assimilated and used only by those experienced on the path of service. In the same way, books on spirituality and mysticism will remain closed in essence to the casual reader; they live only in the lives of those who have moved beyond worldly desires to eternal aspiration. And this too comes by the experience of life, a life of unending enfoldment and pregnant with mystery to those who are aware. One thing is certain: once one moves into service for one's fellows, one is never lonely again—there simply is no time for bemoaning one's own inner tragedies. Instead one gives, apparently of oneself, but in fact of the divine essence within one. That is the way of self-transcendence that leads to the vision of God.

ELEVEN

The Universal Relationship

The end of living alone is being in a more complete relationship with everybody. What on the surface appears to be paradox carried to its extreme absurdity is true if we consider what the substance of a real relationship comprises. It might be argued that a person who spends his life habitually alone has proved his inability to establish, or at any rate maintain, a constant relationship with any other human being. The impediment may be crippling shyness or else such a difficult personality that effective communication with another person is well-nigh impossible. How can the solitary one enter into a complete relationship with his fellows until such time as he ceases to live alone and enters into a full relationship with at least one other person?

The meaning of a real relationship is the topic that has reared its head so often in these pages that it is in fact the central theme of this dissertation on which all other considerations are essentially variations. A real relationship with another person is one in which the one can bare his soul to the other, in which neither will be shocked at the most scandalous revelations of intimate details of the other's life and in which mutual respect shows itself in loyalty and confidentiality that ultimately blossoms in self-giving love. Such a relationship should find its fulfilment and apogee in marriage. Admittedly a high degree of intimacy is to be cultivated during the growing period of shared existence, punctuated by the responsibility of rearing a family and the years of financial stress. But even after many years of living together a high degree of shared happiness, of true intimacy, is not a very common commodity. All too often in even an apparently successful marriage, there is some aspect of the one partner's life that has to be shielded from the other, who will in some way feel threatened by it and therefore seek to undermine it with the subtle cruelty of derision and disdain.

Many married couples get along together more because of a basic need for survival than because of any deep personal love. The shallowness of sensitivity that marks so many marital unions is disconcerting to behold, and it heralds the numerous breakdowns of marriage that are so common a feature of contemporary life. Whether the assessment would have been notably different in previous eras is debatable, but in those days it was more usual to stay the course in quiet discontent and discreet immorality than it is at present. Nowadays if satisfaction is not soon forthcoming there is a tendency to walk out and leave the other party stranded.

The truth is that one's chances of relating successfully to another person are remote until one has learnt to relate effectively to oneself. Until I am at peace in myself, accepting the manifold elements of my personality—the dark as well as the light, the unpleasant together with the admirable—I will never be at peace with anyone else. Until I am becoming integrated as a person, the split-off portions of my personality that have as yet eluded integration into the whole will insinuate themselves into my consciousness and act treacherously against me. Thus I will be fighting an interior battle while I believe I am relating effectively to another person. I may, for instance, relate on the level of genital sex to someone who relieves my basic physical need while the remainder of my mind is preoccupied with some completely different dimension of concern that has nothing to do with the person who is satisfying my sensual desire at that moment. Once the need has been stilled, the person is no longer relevant in my life and can, as far as I am concerned, go away. Thus, in the language of Martin Buber, I have used another human being in the I—It relationship that should be relegated to physical objects that are here today and discarded tomorrow. But we cannot treat fellow humans like this; the retribution in store for us later on both in terms of broken relationships and our own disintegration is terrifying to behold. Furthermore, if one lacks some quality and especially if one is unaware of it, one will tend to seek it unconsciously in some other person. Instead of relating as a whole person to the other, one will be using him to complement one's own deficiencies. Such a relationship will inevitably prove unsatisfactory, and the cause lies within oneself even more than in the other person. One is looking for healing of oneself elsewhere instead of seeking it in the depths of one's own being. On the other hand, when we are centred in the self, that secret place of the Most High, we speak to the other person with our true being, and there is a genuine relationship between us. In this respect neither of us need be particularly bright intellectually or even good morally, but at least we are revealing our true nature to the other. The truth may not be pleasant at first, but where truth is unashamedly proclaimed, the Spirit of God is not far away, and that same Spirit will illuminate the relationship and bring healing to all the parties concerned. Soon they will begin to know each other and see each other's true value. This esteem that we give to each other is the foundation stone of an ever-deepening reverence which will in due course blossom into real love. This love unites the many into one body, the full body of Christ. What starts in the lives of the few will bring an increasing number of people into deep relationship with each other and with ourselves also, because on the level of love we are, as we have already noted, all parts of the same body, all 'members one of another'.

In many relationships a period of hatred may be inevitable before love can be established. The most negative state is one of apathetic indifference, in which one does not care about the other person at all. Quite a large amount of permissiveness in society is a manifestation of frank indifference; people are allowed to do what they will with their lives even to the extent of ruining them with excessive dependence on drugs and alcohol, or by various perverse actions. Nobody cares, since each is allegedly the master of his own life. Frank hatred is preferable to this; at least it articulates a concern for the other person even if this acknowledgement is destructive in tendency. When one's hatred reaches its peak, one may at last confront the object of one's loathing, and suddenly, for the first time in one's life, see that individual as a fellow human being, at the same time feeling human emotions of affinity in oneself. Jesus' command that we should love our enemies and pray for our persecutors, remembering that God bestows his love on good and bad alike, and only in so doing can we be authentic children of our heavenly Father (Matt. 5.44—45), is a counsel of perfection that is fulfilled in the course of a life of prayer and renunciation. If we are naive enough to believe that this supreme work of love can be attained by an act of unaided will we shall soon be disillusioned. If I make up my mind to act henceforth with love towards my bitterest enemy and I go about it simply by beaming good will at him, I will soon discover that I am not relating to him as a real person but am in fact subtly condescending to him. I am not giving my full being to his full being but am eluding a full confrontation by keeping my inner eye fixed on a surface thought instead of looking deeply into a brother's soul, sore and suffering as is mine also. But if I acknowledge my detestation, knowing that it is a wrong, destructive attitude, and pray to God in confession and petition that my heart may be changed from its habitual stoniness to a fully palpitating heart of a human being, then relief will come and a changed relationship will follow. The dark reign of hatred will be succeeded by the illumination of love, as it did with dramatic force to St Paul on the road to Damascus. Those whom the great apostle to the Gentiles hated most were to become the objects of his self-giving love. Harmony usually comes after strong conflict, just as the peace of God which passes all understanding is appreciated best by those whose lives have been rent asunder by turmoil and anxiety. In the same way health is seldom acknowledged as a divine gift until one has recovered from a severe illness.

What I am saying is this, that we have to be honest in our relationships. Honesty requires the discipline of awareness to hear what the Holy Spirit is saying to us in the depths of our being. He speaks to us unequivocally in the sacrament of the present moment, so that we are in no doubt about our basic motivations or our attitudes to other people. Jesus had the same effect: in his presence the other person showed himself as he really was, the aspiration that lay hidden in the tax-gatherer and the prostitute no less than the hatred and jealousy that disfigured the piety of many religious observers. This was because Jesus, like all holy people, was transparent, and in his transparency the grime and filth in the other's personality was fully revealed. It could be cleansed according to the will of the person concerned, but pride occluded the radiance of God from penetrating the souls of the hypocrites and the religious bigots, as it does today also.

When one lives alone one cannot evade this penetrating blast of God's Spirit. As a result one really does begin to know oneself, and then it becomes easier to know other people. When the power of God has come to us and we know we are loved by him and are made lovable by him, only then can we flow out to other people without shame or base motives. We know that the priceless gift we have to offer is in fact ourself, imperfect no doubt but incontrovertibly unique. We do not have to display exceptional gifts or talents, wealth or social eminence, physical attractiveness or intellectual brilliance. These may be additional graces but none of them gives us peace and joy; God alone fulfils this purpose. The one thing needful, that Mary possessed and her obsessively busy sister Martha lacked, was stillness to hear the word of God (Luke 10.38—42). When one is alone the word comes to us loud and clear, and at last we can give up our time to listen and obey. Once we have heard God, we can begin to hear what our fellows are saying. One can indeed relate effectively to other people only when one has related to God and to oneself. To be at home with God and in oneself makes one constantly available to other people also. The heavenly guest within welcomes each weary traveller on the way of life. 'Come to me, all whose work is hard, whose load is heavy, and I will give you relief. Bend your necks to my yoke, and learn from me, for I am gentle and humble-hearted; and your souls will find relief. For my yoke is good to bear, my load is light' (Matt. 11.28—30). The yoke of Christ is in fact the burden of all creation that groans as if in the pangs of childbirth, but in him the weight becomes bearable and the pain is invested with visionary hope. It is in this spirit that a full relationship can be established with another person, for God is there too and his Spirit sustains all who are involved.

These great spiritual truths that are at the heart of an enduring relationship find their fruition best in the soul of the person who has striven long on his own, and has had to bear the pangs of doubt, fear and disappointment without the glib reassurances that flow from the lips of the worldly-wise. These have never faced the inroads of desolation or failure, and their advice is as shallow as their lives are superficial. They see with the hooded eye: one that is shielded by a comfortable attitude to life from anything that would tend to disturb the uneasy equilibrium on which their existence is based. The same criticism of smooth superficiality can be levelled at many conventionally religious people who believe they have the complete truth but cannot face the searing implications of a full commitment to God in prayer and to their fellow men in service. How many say 'Lord, Lord' while failing to do the will of God! They will not enter the Kingdom of Heaven (Matt. 7.21). The Kingdom is above all else one of intimate relationship with one's fellows through a participation of loving openness with God. The peace of God that passes all understanding is one of wholeness of personality so that we can enjoy all the good things that God has given us in his company through eternal union. Once the conflicting elements in our own personality have been brought together and healed, we can enter into a healing relationship with our neighbours, with all created things, and finally with the whole universe through the integrating power of God's love for us all. The mystic knows of the divine harmony that sustains the heart of the universe, bringing together the surface conflicts into a synthesis of reconciliation and dedication to God. We in our lesser awareness realize this synthesis in our own personality as God redeems what was split off and perverse. And then we can relate in wonder with our fellow men. Heaven is like a clear crystal, transparent and self-revealing. In it nothing lies hidden; when we enter we are accepted for what we are. The wounds we have borne that have scarred our personalities now assume the beauty of something holy, as the wounds of the crucified Lord are the object of our special veneration and love whenever we follow him through agony to triumph, through crucifixion to resurrection.

The end of living alone is the regeneration of the personality, so that even if one is on one's own one is no longer alone in the world. Man was never meant to be alone, but when we disregard the divine law through human greed, as portrayed symbolically in the story of the Fall in Genesis 3, we have to grow painfully into self-knowledge and self-transcendence. Only then can we give of ourselves unreservedly to our fellows in a true relationship. The qualities of a loving relationship are trust, loyalty, and the willingness to give of oneself freely and without desire for recompense. There is indeed only one reward worth its name, and that is love. All else is illusory. Through the way of service and the gift of being available to many others that is often less open to the person limited by family relationships, the one who lives alone can, and indeed should, become the centre of an ever-increasing number of people. These come at first for help, but later stay and offer themselves for a greater service to their fellows. These people may well form the nucleus of a beloved community; at all events they begin to assume the qualities of true friends rather than casual acquaintances: as we noted previously, the qualities of friendship are trust with its reverse side of loyalty together with the giving of oneself to help the other person. Such a friend is a rare being; that is why, even if we have two or three real friends, we should regard ourselves as fortunate. To have around one those who will respect one's secrets and guard one's private life is the basis of practical friendship. Eventually this loving community will be an inseparable part of one's life, so that nothing private need be guarded and all secrets are part of the knowledge of our friends. Then we will be in the divine company, 'to whom all hearts are open, all desires known and from whom no secrets are hidden'. In other words a true relationship depends on the absolute freedom of all its members to be themselves. This freedom flows out to the wide world and embraces all manner of human beings with acceptance and love.

It was in this spirit that Jesus widened the concept of family. It is recorded that early in his ministry his mother and brothers came to fetch him while he was at work amongst the common people. He replied, 'Who is my mother? Who are my brothers?' And looking round at those who were sitting in the circle about him he said: 'Here are my mother and my brothers. Whoever does the will of God is my brother, my sister, my mother' (Mark 3.31 – 35). The family unit is both the foundation of the civilized community and its ultimate limitation and downfall. This adverse effect occurs when the little family assumes a dominance and stranglehold in the life of its members. It becomes a roaring animal, predatory and vicious, seeking its own at all costs and intent on preserving itself against the inroads of the stranger and the dispossessed. But the family cannot be discarded without serious social repercussions, nor can it be diluted and broadened by a communalism that practises sexual promiscuity so that the integrity, indeed the sanctity, of the individual is sacrificed for the specious ideal of group solidarity. The way ahead is not by destroying the family as we know it, but by transcending its natural limitations. This is done by extending its excellence to other people around one, so that the love and service, the loyalty and the self-sacrifice of real family life may be available to the stranger in need. This was the way of Christ, and indeed it is taught that whenever we feed the hungry and give drink to those that thirst, whenever we entertain the stranger in our home and clothe the naked, whenever we help the sick and visit those in prison, we are doing it to Christ also. 'Anything you did for one of my brothers here, however humble, you did it for me' (Matt. 25.31−46). It will be a good thing also when we extend our understanding of the Holy Family from the rather cosy, complacent Christmas image that now prevails to a grasp of the divine community grounded in eternity but to be realized also in the common life we share in the world this day. These immense insights are especially real to the person who has had to live alone and has passed through the bitter desert of loneliness to the oasis of service for other people less fortunate than he is, through the wilderness of isolation to the heavenly city of unrestricted love for all men. When one has come to terms with the loneliness that is a part of all human endeavour by living alone, one can also reach the point of self-transcendence where one is able to give up one's life freely for one's friends, who, at this stage, are all God's creatures.

This view of community helps us also to understand the necessity of the experience of bereavement in the full growth of a person first to independence of people and then, by paradox, to a full involvement with many people. When we have lost the support of the person who meant most in our life, we now have an opportunity of opening ourself to him at the level of spiritual reality. This means in effect making ourselves more available to our fellow men who previously passed unnoticed in the procession of life, since we were totally engrossed in a selfish relationship with one person only. As we give of ourselves to those whom we had previously neglected or dismissed out of hand as being irrelevant to our needs, so we find that our loved one can communicate with us on the highest level of awareness. When we are dedicated to service and open in compassion to the meanest creature, Christ himself is with us and he brings all whom we have loved with him to us. Some people who have shown hospitality have, by so doing, entertained angels without knowing it (Heb. 13.2). Indeed, whenever we do a noble action or a charitable work, Christ is with us both as inspirer and as companion. The truths of the highest states of being come to us when we are least aware of ourselves and most dedicated to the needs of others. Grace is eternally available, but it is to the person most empty of conceit and selfish craving that grace will be revealed. Once empty of the selfish desire for a loved one now departed this life, we shall be filled with the love of a wider, more comprehensive community at whose head is Christ bringing with him the spiritual form of the loved one.

In this respect I am persuaded that our departed friends do not want us to grieve over them. According to the life they led on earth and the concern they showed for others less fortunate than they were, they are now in a new relationship with God and in all probability learning much about themselves that was hidden from their gaze during the period of their earthly toil. What they want most of us is our prayers, especially if their lives on earth were not particularly edifying, and that we should devote the remainder of our days on earth to living as perfectly in love as we can. In the Parable of Lazarus and the Rich Man, it was the desire of the previously selfish man of wealth, now sequestered in hell and deprived of all intimate relationships of love as the result of his way of life on earth, that his brothers might learn in time to amend their own lives. Only thus would they escape the desolation that was his present lot (Luke 16.19 – 31). While I personally cannot bear to consider any sinner as eternally damned no matter how evil his earthly life may have been, it is clear to me that the state of damnation persists until one confesses one's sins and offers one's future existence to the unreserved service of one's fellow creatures. In other words, the state of being of anyone in the future, whether here on earth or in the undisclosed pastures of the after-life, depends on the combined action of the free will of the person and the eternally forgiving love of God once that person has come to himself, as the Prodigal Son did in Jesus' famous parable. As we have already noted, love can be freely offered, but even God does not force anyone to accept it. It may take an apparently endless period of recalcitrance before a sinner will start to repent of his past attitudes, asking God to be forgiven and offering himself without demur as a living sacrifice for the whole world.

In this context the state of celibacy finds its proper meaning. It is not one of avoiding sexual contact with another person but of offering oneself in the height of one's sexuality to all people. Unfortunately most people confine sex entirely to the physical act of procreation; in other words, they limit sexuality to its genital function. Vital as this is both for the procreation of mankind and the mutual pleasure and companionship of the individual partners concerned in the act, it is in fact only one facet of a much vaster, God-given quality. It is accepted by many psychologists that each of us has both a masculine and a feminine aspect to the personality, but the dominant quality is determined by our anatomical constitution, whether male or female. To complement the weaker side it is customary to have close links with those of the opposite sex, and this should find its consummation in a happy marriage. The basic masculine qualities are drive, leadership, force-fulness, intellectual power and physical strength. By contrast, the feminine qualities that stand out quite clearly are receptivity, service, graciousness, intuition and psychic sensitivity. It can be said that the man builds the house while the woman makes the home. It is a matter of everyday observation that there are many men who have psychological qualities of a feminine, receptive type and many dominating, executive women, thus illustrating the fact that sexuality is not nearly so clear-cut as would appear at first sight. This, it should be noted, is independent of genital sex: the receptive man can be as potent as his dominating peer, and the executive type of woman can be as open to physical love as her more retiring sister. The amazing range of qualities that are found in individual human beings is a constant source of delight, for it emphasizes the uniqueness of each person.

The true celibate is one in whom the male and female qualities are so balanced that no other person is needed to complement them. Such a celibate was Jesus, who in his personality combined masculine strength and feminine sensitivity, the executive power of a man and the patient teaching quality that accords best with a woman. A good teacher must not only be a master of his subject but also have infinite solicitude for his students. He must be able to put himself in the place of a person who has difficulty in grasping concepts and theories; this in effect means that an effective teacher is loving and full of compassion for those he is trying to help. The feminine part of teaching is vitally important, and it includes such qualities as patience, the ability to relate in depth, concern and self-giving. Dame Julian of Norwich appreciates the motherhood of Christ beautifully when she writes of his providence to us, his unfailing love and his self-sacrifice. She says a mother's is the most intimate, willing and dependable of all services, and that Christ showed them to perfection (*Revelations of Divine Love,* ch. 60).

When a married person is parted from his or her beloved spouse in death, it may well be that the previous state of intimate union with one person is now to be broadened to embrace many people in the love of the ideal father—mother who is typified in Christ. I would not suggest that a bereaved person should reject the possibility of another marriage—and in this respect men are more able to make a second marriage than are women, who depend on the man's initiative. But if circumstances decree that the life alone is to be a permanent feature of one's remaining years, one should thank God for the opportunity offered one to grow into the state of dedicated service and love for all people—male and female, young and old, native and foreign—that is the way of the celibate. All this is, of course, simply an extension of the theme of Christ, already mentioned, that one's real family includes all people, and especially those who offer themselves unreservedly to the service of God and the proclamation of his Kingdom on earth. Much of life's travail is here to teach us to broaden our concept of identity from the purely personal to the communal, from the egoistic to the spiritual. The end is the mystical realization that I and the Father are one, a truth to be attained in the mist of eternity as it was shown on earth in the person of Christ. For God became man in order that man might become God, in St Athanasius' memorable words. And when I am one with the Father, I am also one with all my brethren.

The end of fulfilled living alone should be that one is fully available to anyone in need of help or companionship. One should also be available to the unseen hosts of eternity that convey spiritual life to us from the ineffable Godhead. When we cease trying to make ourselves sociable by becoming involved in groups and societies that really do not interest us but we feel it is to our benefit to support, we can begin to attain an inner balance in peace and confidence. And it will not be long before we find ourselves the centre of attraction for many people who need assistance or who are looking, albeit unconsciously, for someone who has a secret way to the divine knowledge of tranquillity. Living alone is one of the most effective ways of gathering a community around one, a community that does not live with one on a physical level so much as vibrate in deepest response to one's spiritual aspirations and insights. Intercessory prayer finds its greatest strength when it is undertaken with dedication by a loving community working together. Such a group of intercessors is not gathered by intent so much as brought together for service, and as they grow in self-giving, so they are opening themselves in greater faith both to God and to their fellow members in the group. As this happens, so the unpleasant dictatorial and exhibitionistic traits of one's personality are laid bare, and one has to face many adverse qualities in oneself and in the others also. One's religion may indeed be what one does with one's solitariness, as A. N. Whitehead stated, but it finds its fruition in one's attitude to one's fellow men. Some group members will claim special psychic gifts, such as being able to look into other people's thoughts or to see remarkable visions during prayer. They have to be guided with firmness and compassion beyond these psychic curiosities that are ludicrously sensationalized by an undisciplined imagination into something of great importance. The end of prayer is that perfect peace in which the communion with God and with one's fellow men is enjoyed, and the ego with its tendency to self-glorification is stilled in service and dedication to the Most High.

The perfect community is one that can re-echo St Paul's

insight: 'The life I live is no longer my life but the life which Christ lives in me' (Gal. 2.19). But this divine life follows crucifixion with Christ — prefigured in the sacrament of Holy Baptism and ultimately fulfilled in one's personal response to the trials and glory of individual existence.

It is indeed an amazing paradox that until one can live successfully on one's own, one will never be able to live as a full person with anyone else, let alone in a creative community. We have to realize that sharing means above all else giving. When we have given freely of ourselves, we can start to receive as well, for receiving is the other side of sharing. But if the motive for my attempt at shared living is to escape loneliness or some other unpleasant situation in my life, I will simply bring that unhealed element into the new relationship. The end is likely to be a shattered relationship from which I emerge bruised and battered, indignant and disillusioned. The tendency is to blame other people for their selfishness and insensitivity until insight gradually dawns within oneself, and one sees how predatory one's own attitude has been. When, on the other hand, we have come to terms with the fullness of our personality and learned to live with it all alone, we can be gradually civilized and then spiritualized by the slow attrition of our illusions on the hard grindstone of truth. When we know we are nothing and expect nothing for ourselves alone, then are we in a state to be filled with God's Spirit; at last we may become an important focus for a beloved community. In the words of the Magnificat, 'The hungry he has satisfied with good things, the rich sent empty away' (Luke 1.53). The rich, in this present context, are those full of selfish complaints, demands and desires. When these have been worn down by the thrust of common life with all its hardships and pain, they will cease to want anything for themselves, and desire God alone, to whom they can at last give themselves in trust and service. The terrible words that Jeremiah wrote to his scribe Baruch are relevant here: 'You seek great things for yourself. Leave off seeking them; for I will bring disaster upon all mankind, says the Lord, and I will let you live wherever you go, but you shall save your life and nothing more' (Jer. 45.5). When we have been brought to this extremity, as many of us are facing at this present time, we can start to live authentically as complete people. At last all our illusions have been stripped away, and we are able to see ourselves in the clear light of truth for the first time in our lives. And then we discover that the only thing of value we have to offer our fellow men is ourself; though of little outer attraction, it bears the mark of a unique creation of God. When we feel ourself to be least valuable, we are usually most lovable, for our frail being speaks of God's care and preservation in the face of human helplessness. Those of us whose privilege it is to tend the sick have often discovered the face of a helpless child in the previously haughty demeanour of an adult who has at last had to come to terms with physical impotence and the impersonal approach of death.

It therefore comes about that the fulfilled purpose of living alone is to be able to live in an authentic and full relationship with whomsoever we meet in the day's work. This relationship is based on two truths: our human brotherhood and our divine sonship.

TWELVE

Becoming a Person

When we view with the dispassion that comes with the experience of ageing the course of human life, the way seems to be from a state of anonymity to one of bearing a special name, from being an intelligent animal to becoming a full person. A person is a realized human being, one who can act responsibly from a centre of will that is in communication with and guided by a focus of spirit. This spirit within the centre of the soul is in continuity with the Holy Spirit that gives us life, sustains us with his healing power and leads us to an encounter with God, when we are changed progressively into his likeness.

Man is both an intelligent animal and a vibrant spirit; the one must not be exalted above the other since both are basic to our common destiny and both come from God. Nevertheless, the end of man is to partake of the divine nature, to share in the very being of God (2 Pet. 1.4), for in it he was originally conceived. The incarnation of Christ is the crucial event that shows us the nature of man's deification, and is our way of proceeding towards it. The gifted human animal moves towards authentic personhood when he becomes aware of himself as a being who has to make decisions of an ethical nature. Indeed, awareness is the road to full selfhood and ultimately to knowing God in glorious illumination, such as is given in deep prayer or infused mystical experience.

The first awareness of human personhood comes when we have to choose between what is most expedient for us and what appears to be our bounden duty to others. Let it be said at once that the second choice is not always the right one, because there may come a time in one's life when a calculated break has to be made from the erstwhile supporting community, so that one sets oneself apart from others and often in antagonism to the currently prevailing ethos of one's time and place. The reassuring comfort that depends on the

125

approval of one's peers may have to be forfeited before one knows the inner satisfaction of doing the work that one has been called on to perform. This is the meaning of vocation, the obedience of the soul to the call of God, a call that leads to suffering, isolation and death of the old way of life, and a mysterious resurrection into becoming a full person. It is the path that has to be trodden by all creative artists and it is the way of the religious genius. But we lesser mortals encounter it in the narrow confines of our own lives also. It leads us out of the common path into a place of seclusion where we can meditate, albeit in material isolation, in spiritual freedom. This is the significance of living alone on its highest level. For the first time we see ourselves in naked truth. The experience may be shattering, as it was for David when the prophet Nathan exposed his lustful cruelty to him by means of a simple parable in connection with the affair of Bathsheba and her noble husband Uriah the Hittite (2 Sam. 12.1−7). Nathan said, 'You are the man'. In an even more terrible context, Peter too had to face his own worthlessness after having denied Christ on three successive occasions; it is recorded that when the cock crowed, he wept bitterly. This awareness of personal responsibility, whether in relation to a past misdemeanour or a future decision that is to have an irrevocable effect on one's future relationships with one's family and closest friends, is the call to unique personhood; it is consummated alone. But God is present, even when unnoticed.

The awareness of responsibility is followed by a determined action to follow the path set before one; it may be the path to repentance, as in the instances of David, Peter and the Prodigal Son when he came to himself, or it may be the path to self-realization through a chosen work ahead of one. In fact the two paths tend to merge, since after repentance and confession to God, there comes the treading of a new path to service and sacrifice of the self in the love of all mankind. The will in its free direction is the action of the soul, for now the impetus for change comes from within the illuminated secret place of the Most High, and it is no longer dominated by inner impediments or external conditioning from the environment where one lives one's daily life.

In the end, the path set before one in the depths of the soul is to follow God and do the work that he has decreed for us. The work has two components: the service of all life so that the whole world may be raised to divine knowledge, and the transfiguration of one's own personality from animal selfishness to the fully human way of sacrifice shown perfectly in the life of Christ. In the Bible there are numerous examples of this call from God that the person might assume the full nature of a prophet; this mouthpiece of God shows his people the way to spiritual perfection through obedience to the outer law of discipline and service and the inner law of love to all created things. The call may follow a dramatic mystical experience of God, as when Moses encountered him in the burning bush or Isaiah saw the transcendent holiness of the Deity in his great vision in the Temple. But the theophany may be more interior, as in Jeremiah's call to the prophetic function. He was told: 'Before I formed you in the womb I knew you for my own; before you were born I consecrated you. I appointed you a prophet to the nations' (Jer. 1.4—5). The prophet usually demurs and tries to evade the responsibility thrust upon him. Isaiah, in this respect, is the exception; he says, 'Here am I, send me' (Isa. 6.1—8). But this confidence follows the symbolic action of inner cleansing effected by a seraph carrying a glowing coal with which he touches Isaiah's mouth.

When one follows God after the definitive call to service, one goes down into the depths of one's own personality and into the darkness of the world. The way to God's service is through hell, all of which has to be redeemed by the love that comes from God. The lives of the prophets are a moving saga of pain and tragedy, seen most poignantly in the instance of Jeremiah, but present also in the travail of Moses with his recalcitrant compatriots through the wilderness that leads to the promised land. When Jesus, who is without sin, accepts the baptism of repentance of John, he identifies himself with the sins of the world. When the Holy Spirit descends fully on him after he has made this final act of obedience to the Father, he is led by that same Spirit into the wilderness to be tempted by the devil, who embraces all the destructive tendencies inherent in sinful humanity and the psychic powers beyond rational definition. But at the end of all this darkness and suffering is boundless freedom, and with it comes love, joy and an infinitely greater knowledge of God than was previously attainable. The end of all strivings for personal satisfaction is death, but with this death a new life springs up like a phoenix from the old; it is the beginning of the real life in God. Death is indeed the gateway to a greater life, and the concept of death need not be limited to a mere dissolution of the physical body. We die each day when we have come to terms with ourselves, passing beyond the thraldom of worldly desires that serve merely to inflate ourselves at the expense of other people, and give ourselves in penitence and faith to God. We commit our spirit into his hands, even as Jesus did on the cross. As we die to the past, so the past is redeemed in love. Even its most terrible episodes are now healed, being integrated into the fullness of our life by bonds of compassion and wisdom. And thus we arise transfigured by the love of God, and are able to enter upon new fields of endeavour. The end is sanctification, not only personal but also communal. And the destiny of the individual is finally realized on an earthly, even a cosmic, scale.

This is what it means to become a person. This great transformation takes place in the silence of deep, often bitter, self-confrontation when we have to face our dereliction apart from the company of fellow human beings, who might divert us from the course by agreeable conversation and flippant pleasantries. No longer can we escape into manifold activities that purport to serve others but are in fact a subtle way of shielding our inner gaze from our own blatant inadequacies. The period of gestation that precedes the birth of a whole person who is to be a source of blessing to the world takes place in the silence of a naked heart. It is the humble counterpart of the annunciation of the incarnation, of the birth of Christ, made by the angel Gabriel to the Blessed Virgin Mary. As she gave herself unsparingly to the great work within herself in the silence of obscure ignorance fertilized by humble faith, so the whole person is nurtured in the womb of inner silence far from the support or understanding of his fellow beings. The deeper significance of a life alone is that it is also a life with God. When the gestation is complete and the period of probation has passed, we can take our place once more in the world, but no longer attached to our skills and gifts or trusting in our own excellence. Instead we offer ourselves as we now stand, devoid of all personal attitudes either of humiliation or conceit but full of the presence of God. When we are empty of self-seeking and full of the divine presence, we are authentically alone even when about our business in the company of all the world around us. And being alone as a real person we are fully available to anyone who needs our help and counsel. Like the Blessed Virgin in the company of the archangel, we can attend, listen, hear and obey the voice of the Spirit. We can see not only with our eyes but also with that inner discernment that knows the meaning of what is seen. In this way we can give of ourself with full intent to whomsoever is in need of our help. We can, like the young Jesus, be eternally about our Father's business, by being in our Father's house (Luke 2.49). This house is in the temple that is not made by human hands, but is the secret place of the Most High deep within us. It is here that we live alone, and yet paradoxically it has within its confines God and anyone who cares to enter for stillness, refreshment and peace.

If, to quote A. N. Whitehead a third time, religion is what a man does with his solitariness, the person is one who not only loves his solitary nature but also bequeaths it without reserve to all who desire it. For from this solitariness issue forth the fruits of the Spirit: love, joy, peace, patience, kindness, goodness, fidelity, gentleness and self-control (Gal. 5.22). Another fruit that radiates from a person who mirrors the providence of God is an awareness of the absurdity of all human solutions in the face of the divine reality. This is the sense of humour that is so necessary to bind together the individual fruits of the Holy Spirit into a living organism.

I am often reminded of the patient of Carl Jung who wrote in a letter of appreciation to him the following:

Out of evil, much good has come to me. By keeping quiet, repressing nothing, remaining attentive, and hand in hand with that, by accepting reality—by doing all this, rare knowledge has come to me, and rare powers as well, such as I could never have imagined before. I always thought that, when we accept things, they overpower us in one way or another. Now this is not true at all, and it is only by accepting them that one can define an attitude toward them. So now I intend playing the game of life, being receptive to whatever comes to me, good and bad, sun and shadow that are forever shifting, and, in this way, also accepting my own nature with its positive and negative sides. Thus everything becomes more alive to me. What a fool I was! How I tried to force everything to go according to my idea! (from *The Secret of the Golden Flower* translated and explained by Richard Wilhelm with a European commentary by C G Jung).

This woman had become a complete person in the silence of inner reflectiveness while she viewed with increasing dispassion the passing show of her own responses and the fleeting procession of the world's goods. Out of all this, the inner centre, the secret place that we have considered in great depth, was encountered, established and brought to the conscious knowledge of God. As God became real to her, so she revealed godlike qualities in herself, especially a freed will that was able to receive and discern each new impression that impinged itself on her consciousness, whether from her own unconscious mind or from the world outside. This, in a nutshell, summarizes the inner work that can be achieved only by living alone. It is indeed much to be regretted that the young are not encouraged to spend a few weeks each year in the midst of a contemplative community, where speech is a precious commodity to be expended only with due reverence. To be able to enjoy silence is a priceless gift, for it ensures that one will never again feel lonely, even when one is of necessity on one's own. It may be in a foreign country or among a spiritually alien society that does not share one's values or way of life. It may be when someone close in relationship has died, so that the stark prospect of living alone in the future confronts one as the only certainty of existence. It may finally be that the physical body fails one or that the senses of sight or hearing, on which one depends for communication with others, grow dim. All these events separate us temporarily or permanently, as the case may be, from those around us, and show us how fragile is our relationship with our fellow beings. But when we know the eternal communion with God that shows itself in silence, we are about our Father's business as intensely as we could be when all is going well with us. In God alone is our rest, and when we are rested in him, we are entirely composed no matter how unpleasant may be the circumstances of our life.

To those who are well schooled in the inner life, who are in fact persons in their own right, living alone is both a necessity and a privilege. But then these fortunate people have passed from the painful isolation of being on their own to the irrepressible joy of being members of a universal community where souls respond in unison to the celestial music of God. The end of a life spent alone is a life freely available to all who are in need. This availability to others is a direct result of our availability to God, whom we know in the silence of self-giving attention in whatever situation we may find ourselves. To know God is to be aware of his unfailing love towards us no matter how far from spiritual health we may be at that particular moment. This love causes us to accept ourselves as we now find ourselves. Having accepted ourselves, we can be still before the mystery of another living soul, accept that soul also, and finally give praise to God that all is as it is. This is the way to an enduring relationship, and as we grow into the measure of a full person, so we take all other people with us on our journey towards perfection in God. Healing flows from the enlightened person to his brother who is in darkness and, as the healing power circulates, so it raises up all in its vicinity to a direct knowledge of God. This knowledge is inward and intuitive, and it finds its fulfilment in bringing all people to a manifestation of their shared sonship in God. Those who have a vibrant inner life with God know that this is the greatest thing available to mankind, for from this state of being flows universal love. Indeed, it becomes our vocation to share our spiritual riches with all, so that they too may realize themselves as persons. As we give, so we, in the company of all those who are working for a world of peace and love, come closer to God. At this point the life alone is the same as living in the divine community whose centre and periphery is God.

To summarize the situation: living alone is a certain way towards integrity, for in the silence no secret can remain hidden from our gaze. When we are cleansed of all that separates us from God and man by the winnowing fire of self-revelation, we can be filled with the Holy Spirit who binds us into a new community. The source and end of this community is God, and as we work within it, so we are raised to the stature of sons of God following the path of the Son of God who is Christ. He is the supreme person.